THE GOSPELS IN THE LIGHT OF
HISTORICAL CRITICISM

MACMILLAN AND CO., Limited
LONDON · BOMBAY · CALCUTTA
MELBOURNE

THE MACMILLAN COMPANY
NEW YORK · BOSTON · CHICAGO
DALLAS · SAN FRANCISCO

THE MACMILLAN CO. OF CANADA, Ltd.
TORONTO

THE GOSPELS

IN THE LIGHT OF

HISTORICAL CRITICISM

(Reprinted from " Cambridge Theological Essays ")

WITH A PREFACE ON

(1) THE OBLIGATIONS OF THE CLERGY
(2) THE RESURRECTION OF OUR LORD

BY

FREDERIC HENRY CHASE

D.D. Hon. D.D. (Oxon.)

BISHOP OF ELY

SOMETIME NORRISIAN PROFESSOR OF DIVINITY, CAMBRIDGE

MACMILLAN AND CO., LIMITED
ST. MARTIN'S STREET, LONDON

1914

58997

COPYRIGHT

PREFACE

In many ways I have been led to think that it would be opportune at the present time if I re-published the Essay on " The Gospels in the Light of Historical Criticism " which I contributed to the volume of *Cambridge Theological Essays,* and if I introduced it with a Preface dealing with some aspects of the question discussed in the Essay which press upon us to-day.   I owe sincere thanks to the Editor of the volume just mentioned, Dr. Swete, and to the Publishers, Messrs. Macmillan and Co., for the permission which enables me to carry out this project.

The Essay itself was written rather more than eight years ago, when my time as a teacher in the University of Cambridge, though I did not know it then, was drawing to a close.   In reviewing what I then wrote, I cannot but feel keenly that the task might have been better done, and that in this or that detail I may have fallen into mistakes.

Yet I am deeply convinced that the arguments I then adduced and the conclusions I then reached are important and just, and that they have therefore something of a permanent value.

Since the autumn of 1905, when the Essay was first published, the subject with which it deals has come with fresh prominence and urgency before the minds of men. On the one hand grave practical questions have been widely discussed as to the legitimate attitude of the clergy towards these enquiries; and these questions have necessarily demanded anxious consideration on the part of every one called to the office of a Bishop in the Church of Christ. On the other hand a theory which resolves a belief in the Resurrection of our Lord into a belief simply in a series of visions, though not new in itself, has received new advocacy; and issues are raised of momentous and far-reaching significance. With these two great subjects I desire briefly to deal in this Preface. It is perhaps well that I should add that I speak for myself alone.

I

There is a type of mind which avoids, or tries to avoid, all the controversies and all the difficulties which are created by the application to the records of our Lord's earthly life of the methods which we summarise in the term 'historical criticism,' by ignoring the investigations of later years. The ambition of such men is to continue and to end their earthly journey in the old ways, and in the old ways to serve God and to be at peace with Him. It is at our peril that we allow ourselves to speak or to think of such with contempt. It may well be that from education or personal history or mental equipment they are wholly unfitted to come even within the sound of the discussions which they deprecate. They are wise, not cowardly, to hold altogether aloof. Yet even with these the element of loss cannot be eliminated. They escape the pain of a discipline which God seems to lay upon their generation, but they cut themselves off from any share in its immediate lessons and in its educating influence on the religious character. What, however, individuals may do with but small personal loss, that the Christian society as a whole cannot do. We cannot stay, even if we would, the application of historical criticism to the records of the Lord's life on earth. Nay, what reason can we allege for thinking that the development of scientific research in our own day is any less a gift of God to the world and to the Church than the Renaissance four centuries ago ? In both these great intellectual movements we cannot fail to discern

dangers of exaggeration, of perverseness, of irrever-
ence, of pride. But both seem to bear in themselves signs of being parts in the providential
ordering of the world's history. It would be
suicidal, then, for the Church to refrain from a
movement which it can neither prevent nor
silence nor condemn. If we can conceive such
a position actually taken, the inference would be
inevitable that the Church feared the results of
searching investigation ; that it loved tradition
rather than truth, darkness rather than light.
No less inevitable would be the issue. The Church
would shrink and dwindle and cease to be the
spiritual home of those who read and think.
It would lose, and it would deserve to lose, its
large hold on human life.

Let it then be said broadly and emphatically
that the primary duty of a man is honestly to
seek for truth. The student (for it is of the
student I speak) must put aside, as far as in him
lies, his prejudices and his predispositions. He
must not set out on his enquiry with his mind
already made up as to the result which he will
reach as the goal of his investigations. He must
candidly consider all the evidence which he can
collect, and he must follow the guidance of the
evidence to whatever conclusions it may lead him.
We must indeed confess that there are but few

subjects—and in the category of these few we cannot place matters relating to religion—in regard to which any human mind can altogether divest itself of bias in one direction or another. But it is right to put before ourselves clearly and definitely the ideal of a guileless search after truth.

In the above statement the right emphasis must be allowed to rest on the words " candidly consider all the evidence." The purely scientific worker, if his survey is to be complete and thorough, is bound to take account of the Creed of the Church. For in the first place that Creed brings before him a human judgment on the largest scale as to the origins of the Christian religion. And, secondly, the Creed presents that interpretation of the life of the Founder, through its belief in which the Church as a matter of history has done its work and gained its victories. He will not, of course, regard this witness of the Christian society as infallible ; but he cannot justly hold it cheap or exclude it from consideration. And few will be found to question the legitimacy of its plea, that a verdict adverse to itself should not be given lightly or hastily or after a partial and one-sided review of the evidence.

Such is the duty of every man whose powers enable him to investigate the questions at issue. Such is the duty of a clergyman ; for assuredly his ordination did not alter his essential obligations and responsibilities as a man. But the clergyman has also a duty as an accredited teacher in a Church which holds ·the historic faith as expressed in the Apostles' Creed. There are in his case, therefore, two duties—one absolute, the other relative. It is a mere truism, but it is an important truism, that this is not an isolated case. It often happens—with a politician, for example— that to primary and essential obligations the tenure of office adds responsibilities which are secondary and contingent.

Commonly, as I believe, the two sets of duties in the instance we are contemplating do not come into conflict. It is necessary to say this with emphasis. For sometimes it is asserted or it is implied that, if a clergyman works conscientiously as a student, he will as a rule be led to question the truth of the Creed taken in its plain meaning. Such a suggestion, as it seems to me, is an exaggeration which is as cruel as it is unjustifiable. Many able and open-minded clergymen have gone into these questions, using to the best their powers and their opportunities. It is true that in the long process of study they may have passed through times of perplexity and of hesitation. But in the end, when they were ready to pass a judgment as final as any personal judgment can be, though they would have been eager to admit that their attitude towards traditional ways of thinking had been sensibly modified, yet as regards the historic faith they would have honestly said that they had not arrived at negative results.

But there is the other contingency. We know that as the outcome of his studies a clergyman may come to the definite conclusion that the Apostles' Creed in clear and important statements needs to be re-written, and that the only sense in which he can bring himself to say that Creed differs substantially from the sense in which Christendom has always said it and in which it says it now. For in the case supposed the student is assured that (to use a current phrase which begs many important questions) there were no abnormal events in the earthly life of Jesus Christ. The man has in an unqualified sense (let us assume) fulfilled his primary duty as a man. He has shewn, that is to say, complete candour and honesty in his investigations. He has come to those conclusions to which he held that the evidence obliged him to come. Is this fulfilment of duty sufficient ? Can the matter end here ? There have been men who, studying with candour and honesty, have come to the conclusion that the earthly life of Jesus Christ is a myth. Such a student *ex hypothesi* is blameless in regard to his primary duty. But no one will seriously contend that, if a clergyman, he could on the ground of the honesty of his investigations maintain his position as a clergyman. Why? Because in the case of a clergyman to the sincerity of the student there must be added the sincerity of the teacher in a body which holds and proclaims a certain definite belief. Consequently the clergyman who has been led by his studies to deny portions of the historic Creed, like the clergyman who has been led by his studies to deny the whole of it, is, I submit, face to face with the grave question, whether he is not sacrificing his intellectual honesty, whether he is acting fairly towards the Church and towards its members, if he seeks to maintain his position as an accredited teacher in the Church. He would withdraw from such a position in a Church which practised infant baptism, if as a student he was convinced that infant baptism was wrong, or from such a position in a Church the constitution of which was episcopal, if as a student he had assured himself that the true form of Church government was presbyterian. And the issues under consideration are graver and more fundamental than questions of infant baptism or of episcopacy.

But a further question must be considered. The man whose sincerity in regard to the faith of the Church is in doubt cannot himself be the judge. It cannot be sufficient that he himself should be of opinion that the position which he has been led to take is a permissible interpretation of the Creed. Even in the extreme case supposed above, it is possible that the student might maintain that, while he altogether denied the historical character of the so-called life of Jesus Christ, the myth embodied in the Creed sets forth *credenda* about a mystical object of adoration and perhaps of worship. While, then, every man of sane judgment would earnestly deprecate anything of the nature of an inquisition, while he would desire that in all ordinary circumstances a man's own contentment with his position as honest and right should be accepted as satisfactory, yet he must regretfully admit that there are cases in which this limit is transgressed, cases in which a view of the Lord's earthly life is distinctly and publicly affirmed, which without controversy is a repudiation of the specific statements and of the general tenour of the Apostles' Creed. The affirmations made in that Creed about Jesus Christ, and the affirmation that in regard to His entrance into, and His departure from, the world Jesus Christ was like other men, are mutually contradictory in the fullest and most absolute sense of that word. Here, then, those who have been called to positions of authority in the Church must ask themselves what is their duty. A Bishop is an appointed guardian of the faith of the Church. From this responsibility, to which he pledged himself at his consecration, he has no escape. He may feel an unqualified respect for the honesty of such a student as a man, but he is bound also to consider whether such a student fulfils his duty of honesty as a teacher. And (to use language which recognises that every case must be judged on its own peculiar merits) it is possible that he may feel obliged, for the sake of the corporate life of the Church, and for the maintenance of sincerity of confession on the part of the teachers of the Church, in the last resort and with a deep sense of responsibility to withdraw from such a student the authority to teach in the Church's name. Such action would without question be grave. It is only a facile rhetoric which could stigmatize it as intolerant.

It is said that such a position involves a limitation of the area within which a clergyman's conclusions in these questions may range, that in a word it curtails his freedom. We fully admit this. But we must at once add that the necessity of such a limitation is not confined to the Church, but is an outcome of the essential conditions of corporate life. Every society which desires to preserve its coherence and its continuity must lay down its principles and its laws, to which at least its office-bearers must conform, and within which they must confine their actions and their utterances.

Again, it is said that such a position involves the danger of unreality, of evasion, of unjustifiable reticence ; that it makes it only too possible that a clergyman should be entangled in the temptation to maintain a semblance of honesty in his character as a teacher at the expense of his honesty as a man. We must admit this also with all the perplexities and trials and perils involved. But we must add at once that here we have only one instance of a difficulty which is almost coextensive with human life as we know it. For it is a matter of experience that among the most serious moral problems with which we find ourselves confronted are those which arise from a conflict of duties. And the solution of these problems must ultimately depend on the man's own conscience and ethical judgment, quickened and guided, as Christians believe, by the inspiration which is given by God in answer to prayer.

But there are other aspects of this group of questions which must not be passed over.

We have seen that no human power can prevent the discussion of the records of the Lord's life on

earth in the light of historical criticism. Need it
be said that in this discussion it is of the first
importance that the clergy should take their full
share ? And any one who endeavours to make
a serious contribution to these investigations
must from the nature of the case calmly and
patiently examine positions many of which are
sure to cause pain and distress at least to the on-
lookers. If with any degree of adequacy such a
student is to do the work which he believes that
he is called to do, he must endeavour to understand the attitude of those whose associations are
very different from his own, in a sense to transfer
himself into the point of view which is theirs
and thence to review the evidence. Consequently
he justly claims a large liberty in regard to his
statements and his language.

Again, at a time when new sciences, new
methods of investigation, new ways of thinking
are asserting themselves, it is inevitable that many
a man must feel compelled to suspend judgment
on many questions about which his fathers gave,
and about which he himself desires to give, a clear
and decisive answer. A period of transition must
to some extent be a period of uncertainty. At a
crisis of this nature rash assertions are as dangerous
to the cause of truth as rash denials. We have
need of patience that the season of ' temptation '

in ways which we cannot forecast may be over-ruled for the more confirmation of an intelligent and stable faith.

Again, at such a time it is inevitable that, human nature being what it is, rash, crude, ill-considered things will sometimes be said or written. Dr. Newman has somewhere described the work of exploration in doctrinal and ecclesiastical matters, in which towards the close of his Oxford days he was engaged, under the metaphor of ' proving cannon.' It is a necessary but a dangerous process ; and in such a process accidents will happen. On the subjects which we have now in mind even trivial mistakes are serious. There must be no disposition to extenuate their gravity. But as we have need to-day of patience, so have we need also of ' forbearance,' that virtue to which St. Paul gives so high a place among Christian graces. Even the blunders and the indiscretions of an earnest and reverent seeker after truth must not be hastily or harshly condemned.

I have ventured already to speak of one side of the duty, as I myself conceive it, of those who in these days are called as Bishops to the difficult and perilous responsibility of government in the Church, and who assuredly need the sympathy and the prayers of their brethren. That duty has other sides. The very position of the Bishops constitutes them mediators. They are to some extent brought necessarily into contact with some of the wider currents of contemporary thought ; and thus, even if they themselves have had no occasion to labour in these fields, they are conscious of something at least of the force and of the validity of the new methods of study. At the same time they must needs bear, if in this connexion I may use the familiar words, ' the infirmities of the weak,' of the simple believers who cling to what is old, and who are dismayed as they hear of what seem to them strange questions and strange answers. It is the Bishop's peculiar charge to guard the unity of the flock of Christ and to keep in check the growth of a spirit of alienation. On the one hand, therefore, as opportunity arises, he will use whatever gift of fatherly counsel is his to enforce upon those who are called to investigate these questions the plain duty of considerateness, the paramount need of abstaining from defiant aggressive pronouncements, which, even if they do not transgress permissible limits, are a needless shock to the general consciousness of Christian people, and retard the time when the new and the old will be reconciled. And further, if occasion requires, he will, especially in the case of younger students, urge the obligation which rests on every worker in these fields to study and

assimilate what has been written in defence as
well as what has been written in attack, the obligation not to neglect the work of great masters in
Biblical and theological studies who have now
passed away, the obligation (in a word) of maturest
consideration before conclusions of a negative
kind are formulated and published which can
hardly but be a challenge to those in authority,
and from which the student himself may find it
hard indeed to recede. On the other hand,
remembering the lessons which lie on the surface
of the history of religious thought in England
during the last fifty years, a Bishop will endeavour
with all his authority and with all his influence to
restrain the spirit of panic, the spirit which now,
as in the middle of the fourth century, and as in
the middle of the nineteenth century, is eager to
discover heresy, and lightly brands a man as an
offender against orthodoxy. He will labour to
secure real and sympathetic consideration for
much which is genuinely tentative and provisional,
in order that men of many types of opinion and
of experience may be able to become fellow-
labourers towards the attainment of truth.

There is not any formula which, if it could be
discovered, would become to us a sure clue in the
perplexities of an admittedly difficult time. A
reconciliation of the new and of the old is a matter

of slow growth ; and neither with the individual nor with the society can we precipitate the momentous crises of faith. Our hope lies in a widespread and practical recognition of the need of a love of truth, of faithfulness to obligations of many kinds, of patience, of large-heartedness, of a readiness to sympathize with intellectual and spiritual hesitation and distress, and of a mind expectant of, and quick to respond to, divine guidance and inspiration.

II

I now pass on to consider a question as to the Resurrection of our Lord which has lately come into prominence.

1. The belief in the empty grave and in the Resurrection of the Lord's Body seems to be historically the foundation of the Christian Church. St. Paul's words (1 Cor. xv. 3 f.) are : " For I delivered unto you first of all that which also I received, how that Christ died for our sins according to the scriptures ; and that he was buried ; and that he hath been raised on the third day according to the scriptures ; and that he appeared to Cephas," etc. Here St. Paul clearly affirms that an event took place on ' the third day ' ; that this event had an abiding effect on the condition (if we may so speak) of the Lord

(ἐγήγερται) ; and that this event was distinct from, and preparatory to, the visions. Further, this event is set over against the Burial of the Lord ; resurrection is the reversal of burial. It must be noticed that this passage, in which St. Paul's mind is full of the Lord's Resurrection, is the only place in his writings in which he directly refers to the Burial (comp. Acts xiii. 29 f.). In two other passages there is an indirect reference to the Burial of the Lord, and in each of these resurrection is presented as the reversal of burial—Rom. vi. 4, " We were buried therefore with him through baptism into death : that like as Christ was raised from the dead through the glory of the Father, so we also might walk in newness of life ; " Col. ii. 12, " Having been buried with him in baptism, wherein ye were also raised with him through faith in the working of God, who raised him from the dead." I believe, then, that (even apart from St. Paul's teaching in the later portion of the chapter as to the resurrection of the bodies of Christians) there can be no doubt that the Apostle's conception of the Resurrection of Christ included as an essential element the empty grave and the Resurrection of the Lord's Body.

As to this Gospel of the Resurrection, St Paul says that he 'received' it from others. To the question who these others were I have given an answer in the Essay (pp. 33 f.). Some twenty years after the alleged event St. Paul was at Jerusalem with ' James and Cephas and John ' ; some five to eight years after the alleged event he was for a fortnight at Jerusalem with Cephas and James (Gal. i. 18 f., ii. 1, 9). In St. Paul's testimony, therefore, as to the Resurrection we have the testimony of the primary witnesses. He himself affirms, " Whether then it be I or they, so we preach " (1 Cor. xv. 11).

The same conception of the Resurrection appears in the narrative of St. Mark, a Gospel which is certainly a document of primary authority. However we may interpret angelic appearances (see pp. 65 f.), the meaning of the words which St. Mark represents the ' young man ' as speaking to the women at the tomb is plain, and it is decisive as to the conception of the Resurrection current among the earliest believers—" Be not amazed : ye seek Jesus, the Nazarene, which hath been crucified : he is risen ; he is not here : behold, the place where they laid him " (Mark xvi. 6).

From the Second we turn to the Third Gospel. It is, of course, true that St. Luke generally follows the guidance of St. Mark, and to a large extent bases his narrative on that of St. Mark. But to draw from this fact the conclusion that, while St. Mark as a whole is a primary authority,

St. Luke as a whole is a secondary authority, seems
to me a grave error. St. Luke, it is needless to
point out, has large sections (not derived from Q)
with which he supplements the matter which he
derives from St. Mark ; and in the most important
portions of the whole history—the Passion and
the Resurrection—he wholly deserts St. Mark
and prefers to rely on independent information.
As to the question what was the source of this information, I have in the Essay (pp. 12, 62 f.) called
attention to the most significant fact that some
twenty-five years after the Passion St. Luke at
Jerusalem was brought into personal contact with
St. James and the Elders of the Church there,
some of whom must have heard and seen the Lord.
To suppose that in his Gospel he relied on knowledge derived from these witnesses is in complete
accordance with the language of his own Preface
(Luke i. 2 f.). St. James, we know (1 Cor. xv. 7),
was one of those who ' saw ' the Lord. We are in
fact, then, in a far better position to say what were
the sources of St. Luke's history of the Passion
and of the Resurrection than we are to make any
assertion as to St. Mark's authority. A strong
case, therefore, in my judgment is made out for
regarding St. Luke as a primary authority, at
least in the same sense as St. Mark, in regard to
the Passion and the Resurrection. And in refer-

ence to the latter, the same essential elements in
the history—the empty tomb and the Resurrection
of the Lord's Body—which we find in St. Paul
and in St. Mark appear in St. Luke with equal
clearness and with equal emphasis.

It is not then too much to say that the earliest
evidence which we have leaves us in no doubt whatever as to the character of the event in the minds
of the first disciples of Christ. And this conception of the Resurrection permeates the language
and the teaching of the writers of the New Testament and alone explains it. Consider the necessary meaning of such phrases in regard to our
Lord as 'raised from the dead' ($\dot{\epsilon}\gamma\epsilon\rho\theta\epsilon\grave{\iota}\varsigma\ \dot{\epsilon}\kappa\ \nu\epsilon\kappa\rho\hat{\omega}\nu$) ;
the constant reference to the Resurrection as the
act of God the Father (*e.g.* 1 Thess. i. 10, Rom. vi.
4, Acts ii. 32, 1 Peter i. 21, Heb. xiii. 20) ;
the thoughts in the Apostolic writings which
spring from the Resurrection (*e.g.* Rom. viii. 11,
Phil. iii. 21, 1 Peter i. 3 f.) It cannot be
seriously contended that these words and these
thoughts are founded on the belief in a series of
visions. They demand as their basis the belief
in a definite event of unique significance and
importance, an event which illuminates the mysteries of man's whole being and of man's final
destiny. The more carefully we examine the New
Testament, the more clear, I believe, it becomes

to us that what is called the traditional view of
the Lord's Resurrection is part of its very substance, the only adequate and reasonable explanation of the mind and the life of which the New
Testament is the expression.

2. No alleged event in history is capable of
verification. There can be no demonstration
which puts beyond the possibility of intellectual
doubt the Resurrection of the Lord's Body and the
story of the discovery of the empty grave which
witnessed to that Resurrection. No one can prove
that the Romans did not remove the dead Body
or that the women and the disciples did not go to
the wrong tomb. It may indeed be urged with
great force that if the dead Body of the Lord
could anywhere have been found, it would have
been produced and the story of the Resurrection
refuted at once and for ever. Again, unless we are
prepared wholly to reject the evidence of the
Gospels and to regard the ' visions ' of the Lord
granted to the disciples as appearances in the
barest sense of the term, we shall admit that
the risen Lord spoke to His disciples and His
disciples to Him. In these communications
would not the Resurrection itself be a necessary
element ? This indeed is asserted by St. Luke
(xxiv. 22 ff.). Cephas and James, who through St.
Paul appear as witnesses for the Resurrection of

the Lord's Body, were among those who had
' seen the Lord.'   Yet whatever the force of
these arguments may be, it remains true that it
is impossible to convince those to whom a purely
natural explanation of the empty tomb seems
adequate.   Two consequences, however, of the
acceptance of a purely natural explanation must
be insisted on.   (i.) In the first place it follows that
the Christian Church, its history during the centuries having been what it has been, was founded
on a simple blunder.   This conclusion cannot be
softened down.   Such a statement as that ' the
discovery of the empty tomb was to some extent
a factor in confirming the Apostles in their belief
in the resurrection '[1] has no support.   All the
evidence which we have represents the discovery
of the empty tomb as preparing the Apostles' minds
for the visions.   (ii.) And in the second place it
follows, as it seems to me, that we must once and
for all give up the possibility of an historical
revelation.   A revelation must needs deal with
those things which lie outside present experience.
An element, therefore, which lies outside present

[1] "Moreover, if it be allowed that the discovery of the
empty tomb was to some extent a factor in confirming the
Apostles in their belief in the resurrection, the admission of
a naturalistic explanation carries with it the admission that
to just that same extent the founding of Christianity was
assisted by, even if it did not rest upon, a mistaken inference" (Rev. B. H. Streeter's Essay in *Foundations*, p. 135).

experience cannot be excluded from a history which is a vehicle of revelation. If, then, such an element is pronounced inadmissible, unless the alleged events are established with a quasi-mathematical certainty and are also incapable of a so-called natural explanation, an historical revelation becomes a thing inconceivable.

3. A belief in the Resurrection of our Lord as always understood in the Christian Church is, I submit, justified if two conditions are fulfilled.

(1) The evidence for the Resurrection as an historical fact must attain to such a standard of adequacy as is possible in regard to a past event. This subject I have endeavoured to treat in the Essay.

(2) The Resurrection of our Lord must have a significance at once so reasonable, so large, and so exalted as to constitute it a real revelation to mankind. It must be a worthy object of religious faith.

It is now more than ever necessary to protest against and to repudiate the use of the expression ' the physical resurrection ' of the Lord's Body (see p. 48). Such a phrase appears to be wholly insufficient as an interpretation of the record contained in the Gospels. It is, I believe, a parody of the view of the Resurrection which commends itself to an intelligent faith. Such a view is best presented in the words of one whose teaching has been overlooked by some of those who of late have dealt with this subject. I quote a passage from Bishop Westcott's *Revelation of the Risen Lord* (pp. 7 f.) :

" The Revelation of the Risen Christ is indeed, in the fullest sense of the word, a Revelation ; an unveiling of that which was before undiscovered and unknown. Nothing perhaps (if we may anticipate results yet to be established) is more surprising in the whole sum of inspired teaching than the way in which the different appearances of Christ after His Resurrection meet and satisfy the aspirations of man towards a knowledge of the unseen world. As we fix our thoughts steadily upon them we learn how life is independent of its present conditions; how we also can live through death ; how we can retain all the issues of the past without being bound by the limitations under which they were shaped. Christ rose from the grave changed and yet the same ; and in Him we have the pledge and the type of our rising.

" Christ was changed. He was no longer subject to the laws of the material order to which His earthly life was previously conformed. As has been well said: 'What was natural to Him

before is now miraculous ; what was before
miraculous is now natural.'   Or to put this
thought in another form, in our earthly life the
spirit is manifested though the body : in the
life of the Risen Christ the Body is manifested
(may we not say so ?) through the Spirit.

.   .   .   .   .

" Thus Christ is seen to be changed, but none the
less He is also seen to be essentially the same.
Nothing has been left in the grave though all
has been transfigured. . . . In each narrative
the marvellous contrast is written—Christ
changed and yet the same—without effort,
without premeditation, without consciousness,
as it appears, on the part of the Evangelists.
And if we put together these two series of
facts in which the contrast is presented, we
shall see how they ennoble and complete our
prospect of the future.   It is not that Christ's
soul lives on divested of the essence as of
the accidents of the earthly garments in which
it was for a time arrayed.   It is not that
His Body, torn and wounded, is restored, such
as it was, to its former vigour and beauty.
But in Him soul and body, in the indis-
soluble union of a perfect manhood, are seen
triumphant over the last penalty of sin."

I do not think that I need offer an apology for

quoting so long a passage from Bishop Westcott's writings. It puts, if I mistake not, into noble words a conception of Christ's Resurrection which, while it closely follows the record contained in the Gospels, is in harmony with those modes of thought which are natural and necessary to us to-day. It asserts as essential a true Resurrection of the Lord's Body. It is free from all crude and all simply material ideas of the nature of that Resurrection.

Three remarks must be added. (i.) It is only honest to admit that in the history of the Resurrection, as in the history of the other events of the Lord's life, we do not claim for the Gospels the attribute of inerrancy. It is possible that this or that detail in the history of the Resurrection may conceivably be due to the moulding influence of tradition or of ideas current at the time. Such an admission, however, does not in my judgment touch the essential character of the Resurrection, as to which the various lines of evidence are in complete accord.

(ii.) Those who accept, as I accept, St. Luke's account of the Ascension interpret it as a revelation wrought out in action for the sake of the disciples. It is difficult to conceive how otherwise they could have been assured without questioning and without doubt that their risen Master finally withdrew

Himself from visible fellowship with His Church and was exalted (to speak, as we must speak, in the language of metaphor) to ' the right hand of God.'   " The physical elevation," to quote again words of Bishop Westcott (*Revelation of the Risen Lord*, p. 180), " was a speaking parable, an eloquent symbol, but not the Truth to which it pointed or the reality which it foreshadowed. The change which Christ revealed by the Ascension was not a change of place, but a change of state, not local but spiritual.   Still from the necessities of our human condition the spiritual change was represented sacramentally, so to speak, in an out-ward form."   So in regard to the Resurrection I at least dare not peremptorily decide whether any given element in the history was not necessary in the absolute order of things but was due to the purpose of the Resurrection.   Whatever else the Resurrection was, it was a revelation of ultimate realities in regard to the Lord's work and in regard to man's destiny in Him ; and a revelation must be expressed in a form intelligible to those to whom it is vouchsafed.

(iii.) The view of our Lord's Resurrection given above seems to me wholly compatible with the truth of St. Paul's assertion, ' Christ the first-fruits.'   It is not open to the objection that the character of Christ's Resurrection differs from the character of our resurrection, as in the light of plain facts recognised by us to-day we must needs conceive it. For we do not believe that the idea of the resurrection of the body involves the idea of a collection of the scattered particles which together at the hour of death made up the body, or that the only real identity consists in a purely physical identity of material. If we venture to put into our own words what our hope is, they will, I think, take something of this shape. In the Resurrection we expect that the antithesis between spirit and matter will be done away and that, for the full realisation of the personality of each man, God will bestow upon the spirit that which in the final world of realities corresponds to the body in the present world of phenomena. Or we thankfully adopt the language of St. Paul, " It is sown a natural body ; it is raised a spiritual body " (1 Cor. xv. 44). " We wait for a Saviour, the Lord Jesus Christ : who shall fashion anew (μετασχηματίσει) the body of our humiliation, that it may be conformed to the body of his glory, according to the working whereby he is able even to subject all things unto himself " (Phil. iii. 20 f.).

Any one who endeavours to speak of the Resurrection of the Lord must acknowledge, as he must deeply feel, his limitations. A cloud of mystery rests on the beginning and on the end of all that pertains to the present order of earthly things. And, since the Resurrection belongs essentially to the sphere of the ' end,' even those who have the gift of the strongest and clearest spiritual vision can see but a very little way ; their ideas must of necessity be vague ; and their language at best tentative, inadequate, and, it may sometimes appear, self-contradictory. One who cannot claim to possess the discernment of the prophet may be allowed to express his misgivings. He knows that his exposition of what with his whole soul he believes to be the truth is in no sense a measure of its manifold significance.

But to return and to close. I can honestly say that I have endeavoured to review the subject without prejudice, and to put myself at the point of view occupied by others. But in the end no doubt as to the essential character of the Resurrection of our Lord remains in my mind.

If the belief in the Resurrection as a unique *event* were given up, for my own part I am sure that the belief in a series of visions would not long maintain itself nor indeed would it prove to be of such a nature as to be able to sustain the moral and spiritual life of the Christian society. But this latter belief, I venture to prophesy, will not commend itself to the general consciousness of the Christian world. For in these latest days it in truth reproduces the doctrine which in the earliest days found expression in certain Gnostic sects— the doctrine, I mean, that matter lies outside the power of God to redeem and to transfigure. On the other hand, I submit that the Resurrection of the Lord's Body on the third day is supported by adequate evidence. I submit further that it constitutes a revelation which truly meets the great human needs. From this revelation the faith of the cultured thinker can draw inferences which throw light on the ultimate problems of the world and of man. In this revelation the faith of the simplest and the humblest can find a spring of comfort and strength and hope among the perplexities and the sorrows of life.

In reprinting the Essay I have made a very few verbal changes, and in quotations I have for Greek words substituted their English equivalent. I have also (pp. 14, 59 ff.) added two fresh notes.

Ely,
Advent 1913.

ANALYSIS

Introduction.   Aim and method of historical study.

Application of the historical method to (1) the Old Testament ; (2) the Origins of Christianity.

Relation of the Gospels to the Gospel.

The documents (the Four Gospels).

I. The record of our Lord's sayings.

Their preservation conditioned by three influences : (1) memory ; (2) translation ; (3) the editor's hand.

Conclusions.

II. The record of our Lord's life on earth.

Light thrown by the comparative study of the Gospels on their character as historical witnesses.

(I.) The Resurrection. Evidence of (1) St. Paul ; (2) The Gospels. Consideration of objections : (i.) The accounts formless and inconsistent ; (ii.) The Gospels at variance as to *time* and *place* ; (iii.) The disciples unscientific.

Other considerations : (i.) Christ's character ; (ii.) The sequel of the Resurrection.

Conclusions.

(II.) The Miracles. Present state of the question. Considerations now urged : (1) Two classes of miracles (works of healing ; nature-miracles) ; (2) Analogy of miracles in other religious movements.

Considerations urged in this Essay : (1) Character of the earliest Gospel ; (2) Nature-miracles in the earliest Evangelical stratum ; (3) Absence of reference to our Lord's miracles in the Epistles ; (4) Scope and motive of the miracles.

Do miracles involve the suspension of natural laws ? Conclusions.

(III.) The Virgin-birth. The evidence differs from that of the Resurrection.

Sources of information open to the writers of the First and Third Gospels.

Discrepancies between the two accounts.

Consideration of important points in the two accounts.

Review of theories as to the genesis of the history in (i.) Gentile-Christian circles ; (ii.) Jewish circles : (a) Isa. vii. 14 ; (b) Philo's allegories ; (c) The history of Isaac's birth.

A priori expectations as to the mode of the Incarnation irrelevant.

Conclusions.

Conclusions.   Effect of historical criticism on Christian belief : (i.) Desire for truth ; (ii.) Varying degrees of certitude ; (iii.) Faith, not demonstration. Danger of alienation. The mutual duties of ' simple Christians ' and students.

THE GOSPELS IN THE LIGHT OF HISTORICAL CRITICISM

THE title of this Essay brings us face to face with a group of problems which are felt to be of increasing importance to every thoughtful Christian. Many of the questions which are most vehemently discussed among religious people do but ruffle the surface of the Church's life. These affect permanently its deepest currents. The burden of dealing with them seems to be laid on this generation. They cannot be disposed of by the easy method of dogmatic assertion. They clearly demand long and patient consideration on the part of many students, regarding them from different points of view, and bringing to bear on them varied experience and knowledge. Yet probably no one approaches the subject free from bias, either the bias which springs from a tendency (however acquired) to question, or the bias which springs from a tendency (however acquired) to affirm, traditional views. In the providence of God both types of students may serve the cause of truth. The one is an effective witness against a slothful acquiescence in what has been received. The other offers a protest always needful against that temper of mind, a parody of intellectual candour, which with inconsiderate haste catches at the new. Progress towards truth is attained by the correction of inherited views of truth. And this process of correction from its very nature must be slow and painful and tentative.

From what has been said it will be clear that my aim here is not to attempt anything like a final verdict on these momentous questions. Nor, within the necessarily narrow limits of an essay, will that minute discussion of details be possible which is essential for a full and complete treatment of the subject. It must be sufficient to indicate the conditions of the problem, to state principles, and to offer in regard to certain aspects of the whole problem such a solution, however proximate and provisional, as the evidence at our disposal seems to warrant.

The study of history has now become a science, both in regard to its aim and in regard to its method. An historian of the old school was content to glean from his authorities a picturesque, or a majestic, or an instructive story. Finished pictures of events, life-like portraits of great men, the interpretation of the past as a prophecy of the present—such was the work on which he spent his strength. But it lacked the security which comes from the recognition of clearly defined principles and of a single aim. In a word, the historian was lost in the politician or in the man of letters. The historian of to-day, on the other hand, is primarily a student pledged to the work of research. His method is precise. He conscientiously collects his authorities ; he analyses them ; he compares them ; he weighs them in the balances of his critical judgment. From a consideration of the evidence which he has accumulated, he reconstructs the life not only of the period with which he is dealing, but also of that to which his authorities belong ; and in the light of this reconstruction he estimates the value of the accounts, whether contemporary or traditional, on which he bases his results. Thus chronicles become documents—a term which itself suggests severe and prosaic repression ; and these he interprets and reduces, so far as he can, to their original elements of fact and romance. Further, if he is dealing with an early period, especially if questions of social custom or religious belief are involved, he claims the aid of anthropology.

And if the historian's methods are thus precise,
so his final aim is simple. It is not grandeur, or
pathos, or artistic beauty, but historical truth.
Truth is the one and only thing which it is his
business to discover and to present—words which
were really spoken, events which really happened
and which became the cause of events that followed
them. At the same time it must ever be remem-
bered that, from the very nature of the evidence
from which the historian draws his conclusions as
to a distant past, he must be content with probable
results. In historical studies demonstration is
impossible.

It may be truly said that such a rigid method
of historical enquiry involves loss. In this
attempt to get back to the bare truth of the past
we surrender much that is beautiful. We gain
only a relative accuracy : we sacrifice poetry. It
must sometimes seem to us that

> " Our meddling intellect
> Misshapes the beauteous forms of things :
> We murder to dissect."

Yet here, as elsewhere, we believe that time will
redress the seeming wrong ; that truth, at least
the whole-hearted search for truth, has in the end
some better things in store than any of which it
threatens to rob us. Science in the province of
history works on in the belief that in due season

there will come a great reward in pure and trustworthy knowledge.

A few years ago attention was concentrated on the application of historical criticism to the literature of the Old Testament. To speak broadly, calmness has now succeeded panic. A feeling of antipathy and dismay has given place to a sense of reassurance and hope. It would be too much to say that earnest and thoughtful men are in complete agreement as to the results of Old Testament criticism. But at least something like a consensus of opinion has been attained. A large number of serious and devout Christians thankfully allow that methods of investigation which seemed at first to threaten revolution have in truth taught them fruitful and abiding lessons. Such men do not think of the early chapters of Genesis as their fathers thought. Their views as to the way in which God unfolded Himself to Israel and through Israel to the world, and as to the historical character of some portions of the literature of the Old Testament, have been sensibly modified ; and this modification has been found to remove many ancient stumbling-blocks in the way of an intelligent faith.

It was not difficult to foresee that the time would soon come when in a new sense and with a new cogency the principles of historical criticism would be applied to the origins of Christianity. Christianity is an historical religion ; a religion, that is, which, though it must needs be tested by present human experience, yet as a matter of fact is based neither on philosophical speculations nor on spiritual intuitions, but on alleged events, the events of the earthly life of the Lord Jesus Christ. The record of these events is contained *for us* in the literature of the New Testament, and of course above all in the Gospels.

The relation of the Gospels to the Gospel is obvious ; but it is worth while explicitly to state it. The Gospels were not the source of the forces which, to speak of course from the historian's point of view, created the life of the Church. They were themselves the outcome of that life. The Christian Society existed before the Gospels, and *essentially* is independent of them. The faith of that Society has been watered and matured by the devout study of the Gospels ; but it was not planted by that study. The evidence of those Epistles of St. Paul the genuineness of which is not impugned by serious critics leaves no possibility for doubt that the alleged facts about the Lord, which are the essence of the Christian faith to-day, were also the substance of the message which was proclaimed by the first Christian missionaries. It cannot be maintained that this

Gospel was the creation of the genius of St. Paul. The Church was in existence before his apostolate ; for he tells us that he had himself persecuted it. And those who were Apostles before him, as he explicitly asserts, proclaimed in the same way as he himself the Lord's death and the Lord's Resurrection (1 Cor. xv. 3-11). In this connexion the evidence of the Epistle to the Romans is of special importance. The Church at Rome included among its members many personal friends of St. Paul ; but it was not a Pauline Church. The precise circumstances of its origin are lost in obscurity. It no doubt gradually grew up, as converts, whether Jews or Gentiles, found their way to the capital of the Empire from centres of trade where the Gospel had been already preached. If any Church, surely the Church at Rome represented the average belief of the Apostolic age. But in writing to this Church which owned no Apostle as its evangelist or its teacher, which sprang up we know not how, St. Paul refers to the great *momenta* of the life of Christ—His human birth, His redemptive death, His Resurrection—not as matters which were unfamiliar and which needed explanation, but as facts a knowledge of which he could as a matter of course assume on the part of all who were members of a Christian Church. Thus the belief in the birth, the crucifixion, the

Resurrection of the Lord, and the conviction that He stood in an absolutely unique relation to God are shewn to have been universal and (in the strictest sense of the word) primitive. The faith of the Christian Church was prior to, and independent of, the Gospels. And it must be added, however far from practical issues the statement may be, that, as the Gospels were not necessary for the genesis of the Church, so the discovery that they were unhistorical in their presentation even of important elements in our Lord's life would not of itself cause the dissolution of the Church. The Eucharist, the Christian Sunday, the existence of the Christian Church itself are evidences of Christ's earthly life, of His death and of the view which His first followers took of His death, and lastly of a belief in the Resurrection which can only have originated in the days which immediately followed His Crucifixion.[1] Let us then for the sake of argument imagine a result, which I am deeply convinced that sober criticism will never bring about; let us suppose that Christian men have been obliged to surrender their trust in the Gospels as substantially true records of the Lord's life on earth. They have become unspeakably poorer; the historical Christ is for them a thin and unsubstantial figure; but

[1] See Salmon, *Non-miraculous Christianity*, pp. 13 f.

Christ Himself, as the One who died for their sins and rose again from the dead, has not been taken from them.

The application of the methods of historical criticism to the Gospels is a process which we cannot ignore or hinder. It will rather be welcomed by all who believe in the providential ordering of the intellectual advance of the world, and who are convinced that the Holy Spirit is to-day sent forth to guide the mental activity of seekers after truth. Such men will regard with honest sympathy and appreciation, albeit with vigilant caution, the handling of the records of our Lord's life on earth that is based on those methods of investigation which during the last few years have proved fruitful of result in other fields of enquiry

The first duty of historical criticism is to examine the documents which it recognises as the authorities for any period. It is still busily at work on the records contained in the New Testament. In regard to the comparative study of the Gospels it would be obviously premature to speak of final and comprehensive results. But certain conclusions seem already established beyond the reach of reasonable doubt. If I may summarize a large and intricate subject, they are these.

(1) In the First and Third Gospels we can trace
two chief strata corresponding to what appear to
be the two main sources, whether written or oral.
The one of these, in the main identical with the
Second Gospel, contains the story of the Lord's
Baptism, His ministry in Galilee, the last week at
Jerusalem, the Passion, and the discovery of the
empty tomb. The other comprehends sayings
and discourses of the Lord. (2) The authors of
these two Gospels arranged and edited the materials
on which they severally worked, sometimes interpreting them, sometimes giving them new point
and fulness, sometimes adding information which,
as we may believe, either one of them derived
from some authority unknown to, or unused by,
the other. (3) The sources themselves, in the
period which elapsed before we have knowledge
of them, must have been gradually taking shape ;
and this process of formation must have been
analogous to the process of editing which we can
discern in the First and Third Gospels, when we
compare them with the Second. (4) The Fourth
Gospel stands apart from the Synoptic Gospels.
It appears to presuppose them, to supplement
them, and sometimes to correct them. It opens
with a theological statement as to the Word of
God, and as to the Incarnation of the Word ; and
the earthly life of our Lord is presented to us in a

form which explains and vindicates this position. The writer, whom the Church from the second century onwards has identified with St. John, tells the story of the Lord's works, and records His words, not on the authority of others, but as one who himself had ' seen and believed.' (5) If a question be asked in regard to the date of the Gospels, the general answer may be given that the average opinion of scholars places the date of the Synoptic Gospels in the decade immediately preceding, or in the decade and a half immediately following, the Destruction of Jerusalem, and assigns the Fourth Gospel to the last fifteen years of the first century, though those who abandon the Johannine authorship commonly consider that it belongs to the first two decades of the second century.[1]

The traditions as to the First Gospel are meagre and obscure, and we can make no positive assertion as to its authorship and early history.

The Second Gospel, according to what appears to be a trustworthy tradition, was written for Roman readers by John Mark, the companion

[1] In regard to the Synoptic Gospels I am referring to the opinions of what may be termed the moderately conservative school. A useful table giving a conspectus of opinions will be found in Moffatt, *The Historical New Testament*, ed. 2, p. 273.

and '[interpreter' of St. Peter, and embodies the substance of that Apostle's reminiscences of his Master's works and words.

There is much internal evidence which confirms, and (so far as I can see) no internal evidence which leads us to question, the constant tradition of the Church, which we can trace back to the last quarter of the second century, that the Acts and consequently the Third Gospel also were the work of St. Luke, the companion of St. Paul.[1] We learn from an incidental notice in the Acts (xxi. 15 ff.) that the author of the Book, in company with St. Paul, visited Jerusalem some twenty-five years after the Crucifixion, that he became known to St. James and to the Elders of the Church there, many of whom must have seen and heard the Lord. Further, since he went to Jerusalem with St. Paul and, after the latter's two years' imprisonment at Caesarea, embarked with him from that port on the voyage to Rome, it is a fair inference that he spent the whole or some portion of those two years in Palestine and in Jerusalem. I may perhaps be forgiven for adding my own view as to the chronological relation of St. Luke's two

[1] I may be allowed to refer to my Hulsean Lectures, *The Credibility of the Book of the Acts of the Apostles*, pp. 9 ff.; and now (1913) also to Professor Harnack's *Luke the Physician, the Author of the Third Gospel and the Acts of the Apostles* (Eng. Trans.).

Books. It is, so far as I know, universally assumed
that the Gospel was written first, and afterwards
at some later date the Acts.   It is of course true
that the respective subjects of the two treatises
determined their relative order, the Gospel, the
' first treatise,' dealing with the earlier and
creative period, the Acts, the ' second treatise,'
treating of the later and secondary period.   But
it by no means follows that the two Books were
planned and composed in this order.   The probabilities are, I think, in the other direction.   As
early as the time when he wrote the Epistle to the
Galatians, St. Paul was fully aware of the necessity
for some authoritative statement as to the main
facts of his own life, and especially as to his
relation to the Apostles at Jerusalem.   The sense
of the need of some true record of his work, as the
fulfilment of a great commission, would not lessen
as the years brought fresh controversies and
increased the complexity of the Church's life.
When then the Apostle was contemplating his
last journey to Jerusalem, with the solemn consciousness that it would not improbably cost him
his life (Acts xx. 22 f., 25, Rom. xv. 30 ff.), what
more likely than that he should at this crisis
entrust to his friend and fellow-traveller, whose
literary power could hardly have escaped his
notice, the task of telling in outline the story of

his apostolate ? [1] On the supposition that St.
Luke had already undertaken this responsibility we

[1] Dr. Sanday in the *Journal of Theological Studies* for
January 1906 (vol. vii. p. 181) criticized this position as
follows : " I greatly doubt if St. Paul ever suggested to his
companion ' the task of telling in outline the story of his
apostolate.' I question whether the Apostle ever wished
his own biography to be written as his biography. I do not
think that we can generalise from the first chapter of Galatians.
The Apostle was too intent on preaching the Gospel to care
to dwell on his own past where there was no special necessity
for doing so. I suspect that the historical interest, strictly
so called, hardly began to arise before the beginning of the
sixties." Any opinion of Dr. Sanday is worthy of respect
and consideration. The arguments, however, which he here
urges do not seem to me to be convincing. For in the *first*
place I did not suggest that St. Paul ' wished his own biography to be written as his biography.' Save for one or two
wholly incidental notices, St. Luke is silent as to the early
history of Saul of Tarsus. He is concerned with the story of
Paul the Apostle, not with the story of Paul the man or of
Paul the traveller. *Secondly*, let me grant for the sake of
argument that ' the historical interest hardly began to arise
before the 'sixties.' But St. Paul's arrest at Jerusalem took
place at most six years before the 'sixties ; and it is not rash
to think that St. Paul, the greatest intellectual force in the
Apostolic Church, was six years in advance of the average
opinion of his fellow-Christians. *Thirdly*, the more I study
this period of St. Paul's life, the more clear does it become
to me that there were many reasons why he should desire
that the story of his apostolate should be told to the Church.
He was now going up to Jerusalem with alms sent to the
Hebrew Church by the Gentile Churches. It was a mission
of conciliation which he was bent on carrying out himself,
though he did so at the risk of his life. That special mission
gathered up into itself the meaning of his whole ministry.
At such a time, when he believed that his work was nearly
done, St. Paul might well take thought that the history of his
own apostolate in its true relation to the work of the older
Apostles should be given to the Church and bring into clear
relief ' the mystery of Christ '—the divine purpose that Jew
and Gentile should be one in Christ. [1913.]

have a natural explanation of the care and fulness which characterize in so marked a degree the last ten chapters of the Acts. Subsequently, as we may suppose, the opportunities of obtaining information from those who had been " eye-witnesses and ministers of the word," and on the other hand a growing sense that St. Paul's apostolate could not be understood apart from the apostolate of the Twelve, and still more that St. Paul's life and work had their root in the life and work of his Master, led to two successive enlargements of the original plan. In the first place the treatise must comprehend, not only the acts of Paul, but also the acts of the Apostles. In the second place another treatise must be written containing the acts of Jesus Christ. Such a theory as to the composition of the two Lucan Books does not admit of proof ; but it is in itself natural ; it gives a reasonable account of the genesis of the two Books ; it harmonizes with the facts. In particular it explains the relation between two very important sections of St. Luke's writings—the closing section of the Gospel and the opening section of the Acts. The history of the Ascension, including the statement as to the Lord's appearances during forty days, which forms the almost necessary introduction to the Acts of the Apostles, is naturally summarized and not repeated at the close of the later treatise on the works and words of the Lord Jesus.

The Fourth Gospel presents problems a *complete* solution of which has not been found, and probably never will be found. What are we to say of the difficulties which confront the traditional view, more especially of the marked contrast between the Fourth Gospel and the Synoptic Gospels? If, assuming that the author of the Fourth Gospel was himself a primary authority, we suppose that the relation of that Gospel to the Synoptic Gospels was designedly supplementary and corrective, we have given a reasonable account of many differences in matters of detail. But more fundamental variations still remain unexplained. In the Synoptic Gospels, for example, we trace the slow and halting recognition of our Lord's true character even on the part of the Twelve. The Fourth Gospel on the other hand in the opening scene of the great drama brings before us the Baptist pointing to Jesus as "the Lamb of God, which taketh away the sin of the world"; Andrew making the great announcement to his brother, "We have found the Messiah"; Nathanael confessing Jesus as "the Son of God, the King of Israel." It may, I think, be fairly urged that a disciple, whose mind was deeply spiritual and keenly sensitive of the mystical significance of words spoken under deep emotion, would treasure what other men of less subtilty and less insight would fail to notice or would at once forget ; while at the same time, as he often meditated on them, the form of mysterious sayings would insensibly coalesce in his memory with the interpretation which in the light of later belief he put on them.

"What first were guessed as points, I now knew stars."

The history of a great movement will be told long years afterwards with the nearest approach to truth, not by the prosaic observer who noticed only what lay on the surface, but rather by one who at the time discerned something of its grandeur, and who as he recalled it instinctively idealized it. Idealization is perhaps a necessary condition for the preservation of the memory of a momentous spiritual crisis.

Very similar is the position which, I believe, a large-minded criticism will take as to our Lord's discourses presented to us in the Fourth Gospel. Here too we may reasonably believe that remembrance was moulded by meditation. But there are other considerations which ought not to be overlooked. A man of the highest genius has a wide range of utterance. The character of his thoughts and words will vary almost infinitely with his mood, his subject, his surroundings, his audience. Can we conceive that less than this was true of Him to whom the application of the term 'genius' is an impertinence? Moreover the record of our Lord's words in the Synoptic Gospels is not an absolute standard. The version of His utterances preserved by the Synoptists cannot but have been limited and shaped by the memories through which they passed. It may well be the case that the higher prophetic element in the Lord's teaching, which was not comprehended at the time, was eliminated in the remembrance of those hearers on whom the Synoptists ultimately depended, and that this element has been preserved for us with substantial faithfulness in the pages of the Fourth Gospel. And there is another consideration to which in my judgment the greatest weight ought to be given. The conscience of men with singular unanimity approves of some at least of the utterances recorded in this Gospel as being in substance the words of Christ. Anyone who has had the honour of doing pastoral work remembers that not once or twice but again and again he has been asked by the suffering and the dying to read to them the parable of the Good Shepherd and the discourses of the Upper Room. These words come home to the spirits of men, educated by the profoundest of human needs, as no other words

do even of those which the Gospels record as
the words of Christ. To such they embody the
thought of Christ. This is evidence which I dare
not put aside as invalid. This seems to me a
deeper, a subtler, a more human judgment than
that of the critical intellect. The verdict may
conceivably be wrong ; but it is the unquestion-
ing verdict of the highest court of appeal.

Against these difficulties in the way of the
traditional view of the Fourth Gospel, lessened
though not wholly removed by such considerations
as have been here suggested, must be set positive
arguments which support that view. On these it
is not necessary to dwell at length. In the first
place there is external evidence, early in date
(*e.g.* the testimony of Irenaeus, who came from
Asia Minor and who through Polycarp was the
spiritual grandson of St. John), manifold, and
(with the single exception of the somewhat nebu-
lous sect of the Alogi) unanimous. In the second
place this external evidence is reinforced by evidence derived from the internal characteristics of
the Book itself. This aspect of the question was
some thirty years ago very fully and carefully
investigated by Dr. Lightfoot, Dr. Westcott, and
Dr. Sanday ; and in some recent discussions of
the Johannine problem the contributions of these
scholars, as it appears to me, have been strangely

overlooked. The cumulative force of the external and of the internal evidence in favour of the traditional view as to the authorship of this Gospel has been lately admitted, and indeed earnestly insisted on, by Dr. Drummond in his remarkable book on *The Character and Authorship of the Fourth Gospel*. With a candour which it would be inappropriate to praise he accepts the Johannine authorship of this Gospel, with the important proviso, however, that this position is compatible with the recognition in the Fourth Gospel of " the presence of a large ideal or allegorical element " (p. 426). This proviso brings us to what, I believe, will be seen with increasing clearness to be the real centre of the Johannine problem. Few scholars in the present day would refuse to find in the Fourth Gospel *some* signs of a process of idealizing. An attempt to gain a clearer view of the extent to which this tendency has operated, this, if I may venture to prophesy, is the form which in the future the Johannine problem will assume.

At this point the subject of this Essay bifurcates. The Gospels possess two aspects. They contain (1) records of our Lord's sayings ; (2) narratives of His life on earth. We proceed then in the light of historical criticism to consider separately each of these two elements in the Gospels.

I

The Gospels contain records of our Lord's sayings.

We have already touched upon the problem which the Fourth Gospel presents in this connexion. In the main therefore we shall now deal with the Lord's utterances as they meet us in the pages of the Synoptic Gospels. Within what limits do these Gospels preserve for us a true and genuine record of what our Blessed Lord said when He was on earth ? It is without doubt a momentous question. Yet in trying to answer it we must turn to prosaic and commonplace facts. The preservation of our Lord's words was, so far as we can see, conditioned by three influences.

(1) There was the moulding influence of memory. The Lord Himself wrote nothing. He left on earth no record of His teaching to compel assent. Nor is there any indication that any one of His disciples till long afterwards put into writing what they had heard from His lips. His words then have come to us through the channel of human remembrance. Those who were ' eyewitnesses ' and who afterwards became ' ministers of the word,' and many others, treasured His sayings with the tenacity which is characteristic of Oriental memories, and which, we do not doubt,

was in this case strengthened by reverence for
their Master and by the divine illumination of
the Spirit. And here it is all the more necessary
for us to notice what cannot but have been the
habit of our Lord as a teacher of men, because
this consideration is commonly lost sight of. A
human teacher who is deeply conscious that he
has a message to proclaim, and who is intent on
bringing home that message to the men of his
generation, does not fear to repeat himself. If he
speaks to multitudes, he knows that his audience
changes, and that, even if his hearers are always
the same, the only way of deeply imprinting his
teaching on their minds and consciences is to re-
hearse it again and again. We may be sure that
our Lord, who perfectly knew human nature, in
this respect must have been like all teachers who
have made their mark on the world. If harmonists
are fatally ready to multiply occasions on which
a given incident took place, critics are no less
fatally ready to simplify their task by assuming
that there was but one particular occasion on which
the Lord uttered a given saying. They take it
for granted, for example, that there was one and
only one delivery of the Lord's Prayer. Such an
assumption is purely artificial. It is far removed
from the observed realities of life. Our Lord must
have repeated again and again His characteristic

utterances sometimes in the same form, sometimes in slightly differing forms.   And this habit of the Teacher must necessarily have had a twofold effect.   It would assist His hearers to remember the general scope of any one of His sayings.   On the other hand one hearer would connect it exclusively with one occasion, another with another ;   one would recall it in one form— " Blessed are the poor " ;   another in another form—" Blessed are the poor in spirit."   This very obvious consideration appears to me to be of the first importance for a sound criticism of the Gospels.

But how was the remembrance of our Lord's sayings preserved in the Christian Church ?   Chiefly, we may answer, in two ways.   In the first place the Brethren must often have spoken to each other, in the sacred privacy of fellowship, of what they had once heard the Master Himself say.   Secondly, the Lord's sayings must have formed the basis of ' the discourses of exhortation' in the Christian synagogues.   We can hardly doubt that the Epistle of St. James gives us the substance of that Apostle's discourses in the public assemblies of the disciples at Jerusalem ; and that Epistle is a mosaic of ' oracles of the Lord.'   In these ways various lines of tradition would gradually take shape.   It follows that

these lines of tradition, ultimately embodied in
the Gospels, were the result of the interaction
of many fallible memories, each unconsciously
affected by the formative influences of daily life
and thought.

(2) There was the moulding influence of translation. Our Lord's words were uttered in Aramaic.
We possess them in a Greek dress. Translation,
especially when it is the work of unskilled minds
and when it is undertaken for an immediate
purpose of edification, in the process of reproduc-
tion refashions and changes. In the case of our
Lord's sayings, translation must have been a
necessity almost from the beginning, directly,
that is, Hellenists at Jerusalem became ' obedient
to the faith.' The comparative freedom and
ease of the representation of our Lord's words in
the Greek Gospels, as contrasted with the render-
ing of Old Testament sayings in the LXX., is
an indication that here we have the outcome of
a long process, and that constant repetition has
rubbed smooth the rough places which must have
characterized the earliest attempts at reproducing
our Lord's sayings in Greek. On the other hand,
the fact that we are able at times to discern the
original Aramaic through the Greek, and in this
way to restore a paronomasia or to bring kindred
sayings into verbal relation to each other, is a

warning to us that we must not exaggerate the influence of translation on the tradition of our Lord's utterances. Such an influence cannot have acted uniformly. If sometimes it is a curtain, perhaps oftener it is a thin veil. Criticism must take account of its presence.

(3) There was the moulding influence of the editor's hand. The attempt to put a saying of Christ into literary shape, and to fit it into a literary context, cannot have been without effect on its form. And in some cases, we cannot doubt, an Evangelist deliberately amended the words which came into his hands. That this sometimes happened is clear from the following instance. St. Mark's record of the opening words of the dialogue of our Lord and the rich young man is as follows (x. 17 f.) : " Good Master, what shall I do that I may inherit eternal life ? . . . Why callest thou me good ? None is good save one, even God." With this St. Luke's account (xviii. 18 f.) coincides. But in St. Matthew (xix. 16 f.) a significant variation confronts us. The word " good " reappears indeed, but its reference is wholly changed—" Master, what *good thing* shall I do that I may have eternal life ? . . . Why askest thou me *concerning that which is good ?* One there is who is *good*." Here it is clear that the wording of the dialogue has been altered to

avoid the appearance of our Lord's calling in question His own goodness and of His refusing to accept the attribution to Himself of what is Divine.

The comparative study of the Synoptists, especially in those passages in which they record, in divergent forms, sayings of our Lord which from the nature of the case could only be appropriate to a single occasion, and the more general considerations discussed above, are sufficient to convince us that seldom indeed can we venture to say : " Here we have a precise and exact representation of what the Lord actually said." Too often in the past the practice of theologians has been to assume that in a particular conversation, or in a particular saying, the very words of Christ have been reproduced, and on the frail foundation of that assumption to build a superstructure of doctrine guaranteed by the sure authority of the Truth Himself. To take one example, what a tremendous weight of inference as to the mystery of the *kenosis* has been made to rest on our Lord's part in the dialogue about Psalm cx. 1, as it is recorded in the Synoptic Gospels (Mark xii. 35 ff., Matt. xxii. 42 ff., Luke xx. 41 ff.) ! But that inference is only valid if we have the dialogue exactly and completely before us. No one would have drawn any inference as to our Lord's ignorance, if we had read in one of the Gospels : " Jesus said unto them, Which of the Prophets said, The Lord said unto my Lord, Sit thou on my right hand till I make thine enemies the footstool of thy feet ? They say unto him, David. He saith unto them, How then say the Scribes that the Christ is the son of David ? David himself calleth him Lord ; and whence is he his son ? " Such a question as, for the sake of argument, I have ventured to put into the Lord's mouth is very similar to the question, " Whose is this image and superscription ? " The disciples who were listening, and on whose remembrance the version given in *e.g.* St. Mark's Gospel ultimately depends, had, we may be certain, no suspicion that this Psalm or any Psalm was written by any one but David. The supposed question of the Lord would have been pointless to them and would have made no impression on their minds. Further, the difference between the dialogue in the form supposed and the record in St. Mark is no greater than the difference between the record in St. Mark and the record in St. Matthew. I do not, of course, maintain that the version of the dialogue suggested is the true version, nor am I arguing that our Lord had formal knowledge on questions belonging to literary criticism. I only wish in a concrete instance to point out the peril of drawing far-

reaching conclusions from the report of our Lord's
words, when neither by a consideration of the way
in which that report must have been handed down,
nor by an examination of the different versions
given in the several Gospels, are we justified in
concluding that we have a complete and absolutely
accurate account of the conversation.

Criticism then enforces the lesson of caution
on all who are tempted to base important conclusions on the exact phraseology of the report of
our Lord's words in the Gospels, and to claim for
those conclusions the authority of Christ Himself.
While criticism confirms us in the belief that the
Gospels preserve for us a record of the Lord's
teaching sufficient for the purposes alike of spiritual
edification and of history, it warns us that in this
record God has not given us an infallible oracle,
from which, apart from the exercise of our own
intellectual and moral judgment, we can seek
immediate and decisive guidance. Few things in
the Apostolic age are so remarkable as the fact
that the Apostles and their companions, so far as
their teaching is preserved for us in the New
Testament, do not, except on one or two occasions
(Acts xx. 35, 1 Cor. vii. 10, 25, ix. 14), appeal to
the authority of their Master's sayings. They
rely not on their own remembrance or on the
living tradition of the words of Christ, but on the

Spirit of Christ to guide them to a right judgment on questions of belief and of conduct.

II

The Gospels contain narratives of the Lord's life on earth.

A full discussion of the bearing of historical criticism on the trustworthiness of the Gospels, considered as historical documents, would necessitate a much wider investigation than is here possible. We must therefore sacrifice completeness and concern ourselves only with what would be the goal and climax of an exhaustive treatment of the subject, viz. the supernatural element in our Lord's life on earth.

The only preliminary which must detain us is the attempt briefly to answer the question, " What light does the comparative study of the Gospels throw on their character as historical witnesses ? " We accept the testimony of a document till it is proved unworthy of credit. We are concerned therefore rather with reasons for caution than with reasons for confidence. Concrete instances or groups of instances will be the best form of statement. (1) St. Matthew (xxvii. 34) describes the " myrrhed wine " (Mark xv. 23) in the story of the Crucifixion as " wine mingled with gall "

plainly in order to connect the incident with the
words of the Psalm (lxix. 21). (2) St. Mark
ascribes to our Lord such strong human emotions
as surprise, anger, horror (iii. 5, vi. 6, x. 14, xiv. 33).
St. Matthew and St. Luke appear deliberately to
omit or to tone down such notices as unbefitting
our Lord's Divine Person. (3) St Mark (i. 34),
picturing the scene at the door of Peter's house,
says that the Lord " healed *many* that were sick
with divers diseases." St. Matthew (viii. 16) and
St. Luke (iv. 40) heighten the description of the
Lord's works of healing, the former telling us that
" *all* that were sick he healed," the latter that
" on *each one of them* he laid his hands and healed
them." Again, in St. Mark's account (xi. 12 ff.,
20 ff.) the Lord rebukes the barren fig-tree as He
goes from Bethany to Jerusalem, and not until
His disciples are accompanying Him along the
same road on the following morning does St. Peter
notice that the fig-tree was withered. In St.
Matthew (xxi. 18 ff.) however " the fig-tree was
immediately dried up." The disciples at once see
and wonder at what had happened. And the
immediate efficacy of the Lord's word becomes
the point of their question : " How is it that the
fig-tree was *immediately* dried up ? " (4) When in
St. Matthew (xxviii. 2 ff.) we read the description
of " the angel of the Lord " who " descended from

heaven, and came and rolled away the stone " of the sepulchre, " and sat upon it "—" his appearance was as lightning, and his raiment white as snow "—we can hardly resist the feeling that here we have something akin to what we find in the Jewish apocalypses, and in particular to the story of the Resurrection as told in the so-called Gospel of Peter. Again, from the same Gospel (xxvii. 51 ff.) we take the reference to the resurrection of many bodies of the saints and their appearance to many after the Resurrection. The notice obviously presents peculiar difficulties : it has no parallel in, or support from, the other Gospels. Few will maintain that it has an authority equal to that of the narrative of the Last Supper or of the Passion. It is permissible for us to suppose that the writer of this Gospel incorporated a story which was current among some early Christians, the origin and the significance of which it is vain to attempt to conjecture. These instances appear to reveal a tendency on the part of the disciples of the first age, however narrow the limits within which it worked, to mould the narrative of the Lord's life in accordance with a current view of prophecy, of our Lord's Person, and of the character of His life on earth, to enhance the wonder of His miracles, and even to include in the record something analogous to legend.

The way has now been prepared for the discussion in the light of historical criticism of the witness of the Gospels to the Resurrection ; to the Lord's miracles ; to the Virgin-birth.

(I.) The Resurrection. The earliest witness is St. Paul. In the first Epistle of his which has come down to us he asserts the fact of the Resurrection—" to serve a living and true God, and to wait for his Son from heaven, whom he raised from the dead " (1 Thess. i. 10). And this Epistle was written little more than twenty years after the Crucifixion. But what was St. Paul's conception of the Resurrection of the Lord ? " Did the apostle," Professor Harnack asks, " know of the message about the empty grave ? " His answer is, " While there are theologians of note who doubt it, I think it probable ; but we cannot be quite certain about it. Certain it is that what he and the disciples regarded as all-important was not the state in which the grave was found but Christ's appearances." [1] I venture to think that the matter is placed beyond doubt by St. Paul's own words. We note in the xvth chapter of the First Epistle to the Corinthians the juxtaposition of the Burial and the Resurrection—the latter is the reversal of the former ; the mention of " the

[1] *What is Christianity ?* p. 161.

third day " ; the assertion not that He " was seen
on the third day " but that He " hath been raised
on the third day " ; and lastly the inference as to
the future resurrection of the bodies of men which
the Apostle draws from the resurrection of the
body of Christ.   To recognise and give due weight
to the significance of St. Paul's words and arguments is to be convinced that he believed that on
the third day the Lord's body was raised from the
grave ; that he believed that the grave was found
empty as well as that the Lord Himself was seen
by His disciples.

But what was St. Paul's evidence for the
Resurrection on the third day ?   Clearly his own
sight of the glorified Christ was rather a proof of
the Lord's life than of the Lord's historical Resurrection.   A belief in the historical event could be
confirmed or rendered possible, it could hardly be
created, by it.   For testimony as to the event
itself he would have to depend on others.   Who
were they ?   Now in his enumeration of the
witnesses to the Resurrection (1 Cor. xv. 5 ff.),
besides bodies of men (the Twelve, the five hundred
brethren, the Apostles), St. Paul specifies just two
individuals by whom the risen Lord was seen—
" He appeared to Cephas " : " He appeared to
James."   Clearly Cephas and James had a unique
place in St. Paul's thoughts about the Resurrection.

D

An incidental notice in the Epistle to the Galatians explains this. In that Epistle (i. 18 f.) he tells us that three years after his conversion he went up to Jerusalem ; that he stayed there a fortnight ; and that he then saw these two Apostles, Cephas and James, and none other. Since St. Paul, as he assures us, undertook this journey for the express purpose of " seeing Cephas," [1] it is a reasonable conjecture that he earnestly desired to learn from him the details of the story of the Resurrection. It is surely impossible to doubt that during the fortnight spent at Jerusalem he received from those two primary witnesses, Cephas and James, whom alone he mentions by name among those who had seen the Lord, the facts which he records as to the Resurrection itself and the successive appearances of the risen Lord. The two passages from the two Epistles mutually explain each other. It is further worthy of remark that in reference to his subsequent visit to Jerusalem fourteen years later St. Paul tells us (Gal. ii. 9), not only that he again saw " James and Cephas," but also that John as well as they gave him " the right hand of fellowship." These

[1] St. Paul had certainly been living in Jerusalem during the early days of the Church's life, and it is clear that he must have known much about the disciples. When he singles out Cephas as the one Apostle whom he wished " to see " (see Lightfoot's note), he gives a strong confirmation of the Acts as to the position attributed in that Book to St. Peter.

facts are of the first importance. On the one
hand, since St. Paul's earliest visit to Jerusalem
after his conversion must be placed from five to
eight years after the Passion, we have the clearest
evidence, contained in documents which no
reasonable critic disputes, as to what the belief
of Cephas and James was within the first decade
after the alleged event, viz. that the Lord died
and was buried and on the third day was raised.
On the other hand, through St. Paul we are
brought into immediate contact with three of the
primary witnesses to the Resurrection, St. Peter,
St. John, and St. James.

From the witness of St. Paul we turn to the
story of the Resurrection as contained in the
Gospels. That whole story consists of two parts,
both of which, as we have just seen, were recognised by St. Paul—the Resurrection itself (that is,
the empty grave), the appearances of the risen Lord.

The Gospel of St. Mark abruptly breaks off as
the first part of the Resurrection story is passing
into the second. It tells us that the grave was
found empty and that the Lord had been raised—
" He is risen ; he is not here : behold, the place
where they laid him " (xvi. 6) ; and then either
the Evangelist, for some reason which it is vain
to surmise, left his work unfinished, or the copy,
from which all extant copies are derived, was

mutilated at this point. The last authentic words of St. Mark record that the women "fled from the tomb . . . and they said nothing to any-one, for they were afraid."[1] There are good reasons for thinking that the First Gospel, which has close points of verbal contact with St. Mark in this section up to the point where he breaks off, gives us in substance the concluding portion of the Petrine memoirs.[2] But, whatever may be thought of this theory, the point on which I wish to insist is this—the Gospel of St. Mark, which embodies the Petrine account, and the Gospel of St. Luke who, as we saw reason to believe, visited Jeru-salem about the year 56 A.D., and was brought into contact with James and the Elders of the Church there (Acts xxi. 18), are clear in their testimony to the Resurrection itself.

Against the accounts of the appearances of the risen Lord certain objections are urged ; and these, or at least the chief of these, we must now, how-ever briefly, consider.

[1] It has been maintained that the last words are in con-tradiction to what is said in St. Matthew (xxviii. 8) and in St. Luke (xxiv. 9, 22) of the women, and in St. John (xx. 18) of Mary Magdalene. But surely it is rash to judge of the meaning of the words " they said nothing to anyone " in the absence of the succeeding context. It may well have been made plain by what followed that the meaning is that the women told nothing to anyone whom they met in the way.

[2] I have given my reasons for holding this view in an article in the *Journal of Theological Studies*, July 1905.

"It has been repeatedly shown by critics," writes Professor Gardner,[1] "that the mass of testimony as to the physical appearances of Jesus Christ after the crucifixion is formless and full of inconsistencies." "Who of us can maintain," asks Professor Harnack,[2] "that a clear account of these appearances can be constructed out of the stories told by Paul and the evangelists?" It is of course true that the accounts are partial and the information which they give is incomplete. There are many questions which it is possible to ask and to which St. Paul and the Gospels supply no answer. But to make completeness a condition of trustworthiness involves a confusion of thought. It is of small and commonplace events that an approximately exhaustive description can be given. The greater and the more startling the event, the more certain it is that we can know it only in part, even in its outward aspects. Some of the inconsistencies which have been pointed out as between the several accounts of the Resurrection and of the appearances of the Lord will be dealt with in greater detail below. In general it must be urged that to scientific criticism, that

[1] *A Historic View of the New Testament*, p. 166. As I shall quote Professor Gardner several times, I may be allowed to record my sense of the reverent and considerate tone which pervades the book.

[2] *What is Christianity?* p. 161.

is, to educated common sense, a large measure
of divergence between the authorities is neither
a matter of surprise nor an indication of untruth-
fulness. On the contrary, when we have to do
with several records of a time of intense emotion
and excitement, if the actors in the drama were
many, if the documents were put into writing
many years after the event itself, and if, in the
case of at least some of the writers, we have no
reason at all for thinking that any eye-witness
was near at hand to explain uncertain points in
the ' sources ' (whether oral or documentary),
we should account it strange if there were no
variation in details. Divergence in details, when
it does not involve contradiction in essentials, is
pro tanto a pledge of truth. A candid student of
the Gospels claims for them substantial veracity,
not infallible accuracy.

An examination of the passage in the First
Epistle to the Corinthians (xv. 1-8), in which St.
Paul deals with the Resurrection of Christ and the
witnesses to it, will bring before us many of the
most important difficulties which have been raised
as to the accounts of the Resurrection in the
Gospels. We will consider the salient points in
St Paul's statement one by one. (1) St Paul is
not here primarily an apologist. He is not con-
sciously writing a *locus classicus* as to the evidence

for the Resurrection. He is not giving fresh information ; but, insisting on the doctrinal significance of the Lord's Resurrection and especially on its relation to the future resurrection of men, he summarises what he had himself told the Corinthians by word of mouth. The passage is a recapitulation of oral teaching. The grammatical structure of the sentence demonstrates that the first two appearances are included in the recapitulation (*vv.* 3 ff. " I delivered unto you . . . that Christ died . . . and that he was buried ; and that he hath been raised . . . and that he appeared to Cephas ; then to the twelve ") ; and, though the construction changes (*v.* 6, " then he appeared to about five hundred brethren "), it is natural to suppose that the recapitulation extends to the end of the series, the appearance of the Lord to St. Paul himself. The recognition of the nature of the passage supplies a complete answer to the difficulty which some have found in the fact that, whereas the Evangelists speak, *e.g.* of the Lord eating with His disciples, St. Paul is silent even as to whether the Lord spoke to those who saw Him. (2) " By his careful enumeration with ' then . . . next . . . next . . . then . . . lastly,' " Professor Schmiedel writes,[1] " he guarantees not

---

[1] *Encyclopaedia Biblica*, iv. 4058. It must be noticed that (1) " then " denotes that a given appearance was subsequent

only chronological order but completeness." It
is doubtless true that St. Paul gives the appearances to which he refers in a precise order. But
there is nothing to show that his enumeration is
exhaustive. He mentions as witnesses the leaders
of the Church whose names were well known to
the Corinthians—Cephas, the Twelve, James, all
the Apostles, himself ; and he further refers to
what we may call a great public manifestation of
the risen Lord to "more than five hundred brethren
at once." Such an enumeration was sufficient for
his purpose. He could not have referred to the
appearances to the women, to Mary Magdalene,
and to Cleopas and his companion, without
explanations unsuited to a rapid summary. (3)
St. Paul's language (" that he appeared to Cephas ;
then to the twelve ") links closely together the
appearance to Cephas and that to the Twelve.
Hereby he confirms the narrative in the Pauline
Gospel (Luke xxiv. 33 f.). The fact that the
grammatical construction continues unbroken to
the end of $v.$ 5 (" that he hath been raised on the
third day . . . and that he appeared to Cephas ;
then to the twelve ") and then changes (" then he

to the one just mentioned ; it does not imply that no appearance took place in the interval : (2) " last of all " is wider
than " lastly " : if it does not precisely assert that other
appearances not mentioned by St. Paul took place, at least
it leaves room for such appearances.

appeared . . . ") seems to denote that the Apostle regards the appearances which he mentions as falling into two groups ; and it is natural to infer that he places the appearance to Cephas and that to the Twelve among the events of " the third day." At any rate these two appearances he places first. Here too he is at one with St. Luke. (4) It is difficult to suppose that the appearance to " more than five hundred brethren " took place at Jerusalem. It seems to demand as its fitting scene some secluded spot, far removed from the vigilance of the High Priests, like the mountain in Galilee (Matt. xxviii. 16). It becomes necessary therefore to examine the account of the appearance of the Lord on the mountain of Galilee given in St. Matthew's Gospel (xxviii. 16-20). It has been already pointed out that here St. Matthew is almost certainly following the lost section of St. Mark. The first reference to this meeting occurs in the history of the night of the betrayal (Mark xiv. 27 f., Matt. xxvi. 31 f.) : " All ye shall be caused to stumble : for it is written, I will smite the shepherd and the sheep shall be scattered ; but after that I am raised up, I will go before you into Galilee." Here the metaphor of the shepherd and the flock seems to be continued in the words "I will go before you" (comp. John x. 4) ; and it is natural to regard the entire passage as intended to look forward to a gathering of the whole flock around the Shepherd in Galilee after the Resurrection. When we turn to the account of the meeting itself as given in the First Gospel, it is obvious that it is related in the briefest terms. The interest lies wholly in the words of the risen Lord. That others however besides the Apostles were present seems clear from the phrase, "But others doubted" (v. 17). The manifestation of the risen Lord on the mountain in Galilee, and the revelation of His will to those who were with Him there, seem to be intended by the Evangelist as a counterpart to the gathering of the multitudes round the Lord on ' the mountain ' and to the great sermon at the beginning of the Ministry. The impression produced by the narrative is that it deals with an appearance of the Lord to a great company of His disciples and with a communication to them, as representing His Church, of His final commands. Though then the identification of the two appearances cannot be proved, there is much to be said in favour of, and nothing (so far as I can see) against, the supposition that the appearance of Christ on the mountain, with which the Gospel of St. Matthew ends (as did probably that of St. Mark also), is the same as the appearance to " more than five hundred brethren " mentioned by St. Paul. (5) The appearance which St. Paul places immediately before the manifestation granted to himself is an appearance " to all the Apostles." Such an appearance is recorded in the Acts, and, as I believe, in the Gospel of St. Luke also,[1] as the prelude to the Ascension. Thus it is a simple matter of fact that the appearances recorded by St. Paul (with the one exception of that to St. James) correspond exactly to appearances recorded in the Gospels. The following alone meet us in the Gospels but not in St. Paul's Epistle— the appearances to the women, to Mary Magdalene, to the travellers to Emmaus, to St. Thomas and his fellow-Apostles on the second Lord's day, to certain of the Apostles at the Sea of Tiberias. The probable reason of the omission by St. Paul of the first three in this series has already been indicated. The appearance on the second Lord's day and that by the Sea of Tiberias were of interest less as vouchsafed to Apostles than as dealing with individuals. The two important appearances to the Apostles, that apparently on the day of the Resurrection and that which (apart from the appearance to St. Paul) ended the series, have a distinct place in St. Paul's enumeration.

[1] In my *Syro-Latin Text of the Gospels*, p. 130, I have given reasons for doubting the soundness of Dr. Hort's theory of ' Western non-interpolations,' and for holding that his rejection of the words " and was carried up into heaven " in Luke xxiv. 51 cannot be sustained.

It is not too much to say that the enumeration in
St. Paul's Epistle anticipates the Gospels ; and
that the Gospels give us details connected with
the several appearances referred to by St. Paul.

It is further urged that the Gospels are at
variance with each other in regard to the history
of the period succeeding the Resurrection both in
regard to *place* and in regard to *time*.

In regard to *place*. It is pointed out that,
whereas St. Luke and the Acts speak only of
appearances in Jerusalem and the immediate
neighbourhood, St. Matthew and St. Mark are
ignorant of any meeting of our Lord with His
disciples except in Galilee. I fully allow that, if
the words of the Angel of the sepulchre (Mark xvi.
7, Matt. xxviii. 7) were all we had to guide us, we
should conclude that we were intended to think
that the Apostles did not see the risen Lord till
they saw Him in Galilee. But on the one hand
we may understand the message of the Angel as
meant to forecast a meeting in Galilee between the
Lord and not the Apostles only, but the disciples
generally. And on the other hand the assumption
that the silence of St. Matthew (following probably
his source, St. Mark) as to any appearance to the
Apostles in Jerusalem means ignorance, and that
such ignorance implies that the appearances at
Jerusalem were a later addition to the earliest

form of the Resurrection story, which spoke only
of Galilee, proves too much.   St. Matthew indeed
only mentions Galilee ; but in Galilee he only
mentions one single appearance.   Can we possibly
conclude that he and his ' source ' knew of no
other appearance ?   It is worthy of remark that
the words " the mountain where Jesus had
appointed them " seem to imply a consciousness
on the writer's part that this was not the first
meeting between the Apostles and the risen Lord.
But apart from this, we have the clearest evidence
in St. Paul's Epistle, who drew his information
from Cephas and James, that many appearances
were known widely in the Apostolic Church from
the very earliest times, and that this subject
formed part of the instruction given in the Churches
(1 Cor. xv. 3, 11).   This last fact may well be
thought to offer a sufficient explanation of the
silence of St. Matthew and of his ' source.'   If
any facts about our Lord were familiar to their
readers, the appearances after the Resurrection
were so.   An Evangelist was at liberty to hasten
on to record, as the goal and completion of the
Gospel history, that interview in which the Lord
laid on His disciples the final crowning commission.

In regard to *time*.   It is often said that St.
Luke places the Ascension on the day of the
Resurrection.   I have already pointed out that

there are grounds for thinking that the section of
the Acts which speaks of appearances at intervals
during forty days was composed, or planned,
before the closing section of the Gospel. But be
this as it may, we again appeal to the evidence of
St. Paul. No one, I think, will argue that the
five appearances mentioned by him were crowded
into one day. The Pauline Evangelist must have
written with the consciousness that facts notorious
in the Church would render impossible any such
interpretation of his words. It is quite in St.
Luke's manner to move rapidly on without
explicitly noting changes of time and place. He
frequently records sayings of the Lord without
defining their relation to the previous context
(xii. 22, 54, xiii. 6, xvi. 1, 19, xvii. 1, xviii. 1, 9).
We are justified therefore in supposing that there
is a break at xxiv. 44, and that the phrase " and
he said unto them " introduces sayings which were
spoken at a later time than the evening of the day
of the Resurrection.

It would be unreasonable to demand as a necessary condition of the evidence for the Resurrection
contained in the New Testament being regarded
as trustworthy that every contradiction as between the several Gospels and the passage in St.
Paul's Epistle should be certainly and convinc-
ingly removed. Of the most important of these

variations I believe that a natural, though in
some points a necessarily hypothetical, explanation has been offered. My conviction is that
critics who come to negative conclusions on this
great subject are in reality much less impressed
by difficulties connected with the testimony of the
New Testament than by those which lie further
back in the chain of evidence. "The great
difficulty," Professor Gardner says,[1] "in regard
to the physical resurrection arises from the unscientific frame of mind of the early disciples,
who did not in the least understand how to test
or to value evidence, and who looked on the events
of the visible world through a thick haze of pre-
conceived notions, which made many simple
occurrences seem to them vague and monstrous."
It is true that the early disciples were, in the strict
sense of the term, unscientific. They did not
know anything of the laws which govern the
world of matter or of mind. We cannot but ask
whether any of their contemporaries possessed
such knowledge, and remind ourselves that to-day
those who have made the furthest advance in these
regions of science are the most ready to confess
that their knowledge is partial and incomplete.
But it is more pertinent to note that, while lack
of scientific knowledge, and of the instinct which

[1] *A Historic View of the New Testament*, p. 165.

springs from the consciousness that such knowledge is possessed by others, may limit men's
powers of observation ; while it may prevent men
from attaining to an adequate interpretation of
phenomena ; yet it does not betray a group of
truthful men and women into a wholesale invention of events which in fact never took place.   It
is true also that the early disciples were not experts
in sifting evidence, and did not rise above the conceptions of their generation as to the spiritual
world.   But it is at least a rational position that
the testimony of St. Paul and of the Gospels
justifies us in thinking that the evidence of the
Lord's Resurrection on the third day was too
positive and too direct to need elaborate investigation ; and further that the thought of that age
could not have produced ideas so majestic, so
subtle, so divine, and so deeply human as are
involved in the story of the Resurrection.   It is
important to observe in this connexion that the
phrase ' the physical resurrection,' which some
writers use in a tone of disparagement, falls far
short of expressing the teaching of the New Testament.   If we seriously believe in the Resurrection,
we regard it as an event in which the ultimate
realities of the world and of life are involved ; it
is a reconciliation of the antithesis of spirit and
matter.

Of two further considerations historical criticism is bound, if it faces the whole position, to take account. It cannot overlook the fact that the Lord was morally no ordinary man ; that He claimed to be in a unique relation to God and to men, and to reveal God to men. And in the second place it must take into account the sequel of the Resurrection. The Resurrection is the one explanation of the existence of the Christian Church. On the basis of a belief in the Resurrection the Christian Society arose and has lived, at times seeming to sin against its first principles, yet surviving ; again and again in the hour of its apparent decrepitude renewing its youth, proving itself a moral power able to regenerate men of every type, of every race, of every age. The Resurrection cannot be separated from the effects which have flowed from it through all the Christian centuries.

The whole historical evidence for the Resurrection of our Lord, critically examined, is, I solemnly believe, adequate. But no historical evidence can compel men to believe that an alleged event in the past actually took place. From the nature of the case such evidence can only establish its probability. If the alleged event belongs to the sphere of religion, when historical criticism has done its work, the result becomes the material on which

E

religious faith works. Faith in the living God
alone enables us to discern the congruity of the
Resurrection, to realise it, and to know in our own
lives its power.

(II.) The Miracles. In the second place we
turn to a subject which is subordinate to the
question, vital as it seems to me, of the Resurrection—the record in the Gospels of miracles
attributed to our Lord.

It can hardly be questioned that the miracles
were regarded by the Evangelists and by the men
of that age as in the fullest sense interruptions of
the common course of nature, and therefore as
immediate signs of a supervening Divine power.
What is our position in regard to them in these
days ? On the one hand it may be said that the
old rationalistic view which reckoned the miracles
as " the result of imposture in the Master, and
easy credulity in the disciples," or else as the
outcome of pure deliberate fraud on the part of
Christ's followers, has passed away. On the other
hand few would now maintain that the miracles
are *to us* proofs of the Divine mission of Jesus
Christ. Their evidential force, supposing them to
have been wrought, was immediate: they appealed
to those who originally saw them. And the conviction aroused in the primary witnesses could

not be communicated to later generations. Thus the problem presented by our Lord's miracles is for us less theological and apologetic and far more historical and literary than it used to appear to our fathers.

The considerations to which attention is now commonly called are these :

(1) The miracles are divided into two classes. In the one class are placed the works of healing ; and these, speaking generally, are regarded as authentic. "Jesus as a healer of disease is historic," so writes Professor Gardner,[1] " and the tales told of His cures, though doubtless deformed by exaggeration and distorted by very imperfect physiological knowledge, rest on a basis of fact." To the other class are assigned the so-called nature miracles, such as the feeding of the multitudes and the walking on the sea.

(2) It is urged, if I may again quote Professor Gardner,[2] that "whether we investigate the history of the past, or turn our attention to the less civilised countries of the world in which we live, we find that no class of phenomena is a more constant concomitant of the story of the rise and progress of religions than the miraculous ; that a prophet will scarcely be listened to in any land,

[1] *A Historic View of the New Testament*, p. 146.
[2] *Ib.* p. 146.

unless he is credited by his followers with the
power of reversing or superseding the laws of
nature ; that marvels follow the steps of the
saint by an inevitable law of human nature."
Thus the so-called nature miracles are regarded
as accretions to the authentic story of Christ's
life, and as analogous to observed phenomena in
the rise and growth of other religious movements.

These positions must be fairly and candidly
faced ; and in this connexion the following considerations seem to me important.

(1) The Gospel according to St. Mark, which
appears to be the earliest and simplest of the
Gospels, presents the Lord far less as the teacher
than as the healer and succourer of men.   In the
portrait there drawn it is the characteristics of
pity and of power which stand out in special
prominence.

(2) We can draw no distinction between the
accounts of the miracles of healing and those of
the so-called nature miracles.   The latter class of
miracle, as well as the former, is found in the
earliest stratum of the Evangelical narratives.

(3) The New Testament outside the Gospels
contains two references and only two references to
our Lord's miracles.   In Acts x. 38 St. Peter is
represented as alluding to our Lord having gone
about " doing good and healing all that were

oppressed of the devil " ; but these works are not in dispute. Again, St. Luke makes the same Apostle on the Day of Pentecost appeal to "mighty works and wonders and signs, which God did by him in the midst of you " as pledges of the Divine mission of Jesus of Nazareth (Acts ii. 22) ; and this appeal is made in the one place in which it could naturally and rightly have been made, *i.e.*, in the presence of those who are alleged to have themselves witnessed the works—" even as ye yourselves know." Elsewhere in the New Testament, though St. Paul is deeply conscious that the Jews whom a crucified Messiah " offended " " demand signs " (1 Cor. i. 22), and though he (Gal. iii. 5 ; 1 Cor. xii. 9 f., 28 ff. ; 2 Cor. xii. 12 ; Rom. xv. 19) and the writer of the Epistle to the Hebrews (ii. 4) allude to " signs and wonders " wrought in Apostolic times, there is a complete and unbroken silence as to the miracles of our Lord. A similar statement may be made as to the Apostolic Fathers. The fact is most significant. It constitutes in my opinion a strong historical argument against the position that in the days when the Evangelical tradition was in process of formation, and when the Gospels were written, there was a tendency at work among the disciples which impelled them to decorate the story of their Master's life with fictitious miracles.

(4) The motive and scope of the Lord's miracles recorded in the Gospels are ever the same. The notices of the miracles are scattered up and down over the Gospels. But, when they are considered in relation to each other, we discover in them an undesigned unity. Together they cover the whole ground of our Lord's work as the Saviour, renewing each element in man's complex being and restoring peace in the physical order.[1] They are not presented in the Gospels as primarily

[1] Two incidents in the Gospels may perhaps be adduced against this statement. (1) The destruction of the Gadarene swine (Mark v. 11 ff., Matt. viii. 30 ff., Luke viii. 32 ff.). I call attention to two points. (a) The man, believing that his thoughts and words were the thoughts and words of the devils, asks from our Lord permission that the devils should go into the swine. That the man should be convinced that the devils had found another home was probably essential to his cure. (b) St. Mark says simply, " Now there was there on the mountain side a great herd of swine feeding " (v. 11 ; comp. Luke viii. 32). St. Matthew introduces a notice of the distance of the swine from the man (" afar off from them," v. 30)—probably his own interpretation of his ' source.' It is likely that our Lord's word of permission was followed by a frenzied rush of the man, still identifying himself with the devils, towards the swine ; hence their panic and destruction. (2) The withering of the fig-tree (Mark xi. 12 ff., Matt. xxi. 19 ff.). Our Lord, noting perhaps signs of decay, saw in the fig-tree a parable (comp. Mark xiii. 28, Matt. xxiv. 32, Luke xiii. 6, xxi. 29). The disciples thought that our Lord cursed the tree (Mark xi. 21) ; or at least this was the view of their thoughts which the Evangelist long after records. Those who do not hold that in the Gospels we have an exact representation of our Lord's words are free to believe that our Saviour did not curse the tree but foretold its fate. Such a position does not in the least degree involve any questioning of ' the righteous judgement of God ' in cases where there is moral responsibility.

designed to enhance His dignity and His power.[1]
If they had been the invention of pious fancy,
yearning to illustrate by imposing stories His
greatness and His glory, it is a moral impossibility
that this subtle unity of purpose should have been
so consistently and so unobtrusively observed.

It is impossible at this point not to ask the
question whether, if we regard the miracles of our
Lord as historical, we must consider that they
involve a suspension of the so-called laws of nature.
Physical science teaches us a twofold lesson.   On
the one hand every one knows that science reveals
to us a universe, vast in relation to space and in
regard to time, in which forces are found to act
according to fixed and undeviating laws.   The
inference drawn from the investigation of all
known phenomena is that these laws are constant
in their operation.   On the other hand science
startles us by the revelation that beneath the
surface of the familiar world there are forces,
hitherto unsuspected, ever ready to operate when
we have learned the secret how to set them in
motion.   And further it is true, I think, that
psychology justifies us in assigning a far larger
province than men once allowed to the will of man
as an agent in the world of men and perhaps also

[1] Partial exceptions to this statement are perhaps to be
found in John ii. 11, xi. 4.

in the world of nature. But we have no experience which enables us to form any conception of the essential potency of a will never weakened by sin and always controlled and quickened by uninterrupted communion with God. This is a consideration which the historical student, who desires to take into account all the conditions of the problem, cannot justly overlook. And further, if we accept the doctrine of the Divine immanence in nature, and connect that doctrine, as the New Testament encourages us to do, with the Person of the Lord, then miracles, as Dr. Illingworth has pointed out, may well be regarded as a strictly ' natural ' element in our Lord's life on earth.

That there was conspicuously present in the Lord's life an element of activity transcending common experience is a conclusion which rests on amply sufficient evidence. At the same time there are considerations to which we cannot honestly shut our eyes. The accounts of particular miracles come to us in records written by ordinary men ; and these records are based on the reminiscences of ordinary men, whose observations were conditioned by the ideas of their age. The comparative study of the Gospels shews us, as we have already seen, that there were tendencies in operation among Christ's followers in the earliest days which might conceivably transfer this or that event across the boundary which for most minds separates the memorable from the miraculous. If then it is unreasonable to maintain that the whole of the so-called supernatural activity of our Lord was due to a mythopoeic tendency among His followers, yet criticism must be free to examine the accounts of the several miracles in the light of the ascertained characteristics both of the evangelical writers themselves and also of their race and age. We have no right peremptorily to decide beforehand that every narrative involving miracle will stand the test of careful and thorough investigation. It is as unfair for the defender as it is for the assailant of the so-called miraculous element in the Gospel history to maintain that Christian belief, or even the substantial veracity of the records of our Lord's life, depends on the accuracy of every detail of every narrative, or even on the general accuracy of every narrative, in which miracle has a place.

(III.) The Virgin-birth. In the last place we have to consider the difficult and anxious question of the Virgin-birth.

In several important respects the evidence for the Virgin-birth differs from the evidence for the Resurrection. (1) The history of the Lord's birth

was not part of the original Gospel. The earliest
of the Gospels, that of St. Mark, begins with the
Baptism of John. So did the Gospel of St. Luke
as at first written or at any rate as at first planned,[1]

---

[1] The position taken up in the text above must be justified
in a note. In the opening sentence of the Acts St. Luke
defines the subject of " the former treatise " (*i.e.* the Gospel)
in these words : " Concerning all that Jesus began to do and
to teach until the day in which he was received up." The
meaning of these words is " all things which Jesus began to
do and to teach and continued to do and to teach until that
day in which He was taken up." For the brachylogy " began
. . . until " compare Luke xxiii. 5, " beginning from Galilee
even unto this place ": Matt. xx. 8, " beginning from the
last unto the first." It is carried still further in Luke xxiv.
27, " beginning from Moses and from all the prophets, he
interpreted." Hence Chrysostom's brief paraphrase of
Acts i. 1—" from the beginning until the end "—is absolutely
correct. What this " beginning " (cf. Mark i. 1) was is plain
from other Lucan passages—Acts i. 21, " all the time that the
Lord Jesus went in and went out among us, beginning from
the baptism of John, unto the day that he was received up
from us " (a parallel to i. 1 which seems to put the interpretation given above beyond doubt) : x. 37, " beginning from
Galilee, after the baptism which John preached." The
proof is completed by the emphatic insertion of the words
" when he began " in reference to Jesus immediately after the
account of the Baptism : " and Jesus himself, when he began,
was about thirty years of age " (Luke iii. 23). Two important
inferences must be drawn from Acts i. 1. (1) The " former
treatise " included, or was planned to include, the Ascension
—an inference which has an important bearing on the reading
in Luke xxiv. 51 and on the relation of Luke xxiv. 50 ff. to
Acts i. 6 ff. (2) It began, or was planned to begin, with the
Baptism of John ; and therefore it did not include the story
of the birth and of the childhood. I have already pointed out
reasons for thinking that the Acts was written, or planned,
before the Gospel. It seems probable that, when St. Luke
wrote Acts i. 1, the plan of the Gospel had formed itself in
his mind, and that he intended to follow his source (*i.e.* the
Marcan Gospel) and begin the history with the Baptism of

though it must be at once emphatically stated that the evidence of style is decisive that the first two chapters of that Gospel are the work of the same writer as the rest of the Book.   There is no allusion to the circumstances of the Lord's birth in any Book of the New Testament except the First and the Third Gospels.   St. Paul (1 Cor. xv. 2 f.) defines the Gospel which he preached as comprehending the Death, the Burial, and the Resurrection of Christ.   No reference to the Virgin-birth is found in the doctrinal teaching of St. Paul, St. Peter, or St. John.[1]   (2) There is

---

John.   The fact that there is absolutely no textual evidence against Luke i. ii. (contrast the case of [Mark] xvi. 9 ff.) at once negatives the possible suggestion that the two chapters were added in a second edition of the Gospel.   We conclude that before the Gospel was published one of two things had happened :   *either* the Evangelist had received information as to the Lord's birth which he had not possessed before ;   *or* he had for some reason become free to use information which he already possessed but might not disclose.

[1] I am, however, convinced on grounds of literary criticism that the writer of the Fourth Gospel implies that he knew and accepted the story of the Lord's supernatural birth.   In all literature which deals with narrative, if it rises above the level of a prosaic chronicle, irony plays a part.   This is especially the case in literature of a dramatic type.   The reader is in possession of facts of which certain characters in the story are ignorant.   These characters, often at a crisis in the history, are represented as perplexed, when the key to their difficulty lies in facts of which they are ignorant, but of which the reader is well aware ;   or as uttering some saying either extraordinarily in harmony with, or in flagrant contradiction to, these facts.   And the reader from his vantage ground of superior knowledge admires or blames or pities. If the writer is a writer of fiction, these utterances, of course,

no clear evidence of a tradition on this subject
in the Church independent of the Gospels of St.
Matthew and of St. Luke. A confession of belief
in the Virgin-birth has a place in the earliest forms
of the Creed. It is insisted on in the Epistles of
Ignatius and in the earliest Apologies, those of
Aristides and of Justin. But it seems clear that
our Gospels were known in the Christian Church
many years before the date of the earliest of these

---

are a creation of his art. If he is writing a true history, his
skill is shewn either in selecting these sayings for record and
bringing them out in clear relief or in moulding the language
of the speakers. In this connexion then we have to deal
with three sayings in St. John. They are these : (1) i. 45 f.,
" Philip findeth Nathaniel, and saith unto him, We have
found him, of whom Moses in the law, and the prophets, did
write, Jesus of Nazareth, the son of Joseph. And Nathaniel
said unto him, Can any good thing come out of Nazareth ?
Philip saith unto him, Come and see " : (2) vi. 42, " And
they said, Is not this Jesus, the son of Joseph, whose father
and mother we know ? how doth he now say, I am come
down out of heaven ? " : (3) vii. 41 ff., " Others said, This
is the Christ. But some said, What, doth the Christ come
out of Galilee ? Hath not the scripture said that the Christ
cometh of the seed of David, and from Bethlehem, the village
where David was ? So there was a division in the multitude
because of him." Now in interpreting these passages we have
to take account of four considerations—(a) that the speaker
in each case is a *dramatis persona* and not the writer of the
Gospel ; (b) that (quite apart from the likelihood that the writer
of the Fourth Gospel had an independent knowledge of the story
of the Virgin Mother and of the birth at Bethlehem) the Third
Gospel and probably the First also must have been in circula-
tion some time before the Fourth Gospel was written ; (c)
that in the Fourth Gospel the dramatic element is strongly
developed ; (d) that the writer at the crisis of the history
emphasizes a notable ' ironical ' saying by commenting on it
(xi. 49 ff.). I venture, therefore, to maintain that a literary

writings and of the earliest form of the Creed.   We
cannot therefore assert that the Church's belief
in the Virgin-birth was not derived from these
Gospels.

It may indeed be urged with the highest degree
of probability that silence could not but be maintained till the death of the Lord's mother, and
that in this hypothesis we have a satisfactory
explanation of the absence of the history of the

---

appreciation of the three passages quoted above leaves little
doubt that the writer of the Fourth Gospel knew and accepted
the story of the Lord's supernatural birth.

There are two passages (Luke iv. 22, Matt. xiii. 55 ff.) in
the Synoptic Gospels which, I believe, must be explained in
the same way, *i.e.* as instances of irony.   It will be noticed
that in these passages also it is not the Evangelists who are
speaking but characters whose part in the great drama they
record.   St. Mark (vi. 3) writes thus :   " Is not this the
carpenter, the son of Mary, and brother of James, and Joses,
and Judas, and Simon ?   and are not his sisters here with us ?
And they were offended in him."   Following St. Mark as
the ultimate source (i.) St. Luke (iv. 22) has : " All bare him
witness, and wondered at the words of grace which proceeded
out of his mouth :   and they said, Is not this Joseph's son ? "
(ii.) St. Matthew (xiii. 55 ff.) has : " Is not this the carpenter's
son ? is not his mother called Mary ?   and his brethren, James,
and Joseph, and Simon, and Judas ?   And his sisters, are
they not all with us ?   Whence then hath this man all these
things ? "   I submit that it is a literary criticism of a somewhat insipid kind which supposes that St. Luke and St.
Matthew altered a phrase of their source in order to make
their characters speak (as the critics consider) quite accurately
and correctly, especially when their emendations of their
source are in contradiction to what is recorded in the two
Gospels themselves.   I further submit that the force and
vigour of the narrative in either Evangelist are greatly increased if the variation of phrase is an example of deliberate
irony.   [1913.]

Lord's birth from the original Gospel. But an
explanation of the want of evidence does not
create evidence. And thus the only testimony
which we have is supplied by the Gospels according to St. Matthew and St. Luke. What then are
we to say of these two authorities and of the two
forms of the story which they respectively present?

It has been remarked by Bishop Gore [1] and
others that the narrative of St. Matthew views
everything from the side of Joseph, and " bears
upon it undesigned but evident traces of coming
from the information of Joseph " ; that the story
in St. Luke regards the events from the side of
Mary and thus supplies internal evidence of being
derived ultimately from her. From a critical
point of view we must regard the First Gospel as
anonymous ; and thus we have no clue at all to
the source whence the writer derived the substance
of the first two chapters. But the case of the
Third Gospel is altogether different. There are,
I believe, very strong critical reasons for accepting
the tradition that the Acts and consequently also
the Third Gospel were the work of St. Luke.[2]
The Acts affords evidence, as we have already
seen, that the writer spent some time in Jerusalem
and in Palestine, and further that he was known
to James, the brother of the Lord. It is not an

[1] *Dissertations*, pp. 18, 27 f.   [2] See above, p. 12.

extravagant conjecture that he derived his knowledge of the birth and infancy of our Lord from St.
James and other members of the Holy Family.
As regards St. Luke's story, therefore, the supposition that it is ultimately derived from the Lord's
mother is in agreement with what we independ-
ently infer from a study of the other Lucan
document as to the sources of information open
to the Evangelist.

When we compare the two versions of the story
of the Lord's birth, it must be allowed that, though
the discrepancies between them are often exagger-
ated, it is not easy to harmonize them.   But the
difficulty caused by the variations between them
are only serious to those, whether defenders or
assailants of their historical character, who postu-
late the inerrancy of the Gospels in matters of
detail.   They do not appear, either in magnitude
or in character, to be other than we should naturally
expect in the case of two independent writers who
edited different accounts of events which had
taken place more than sixty years earlier, and
who had themselves no personal or complete
knowledge of the facts, and, when they wrote, were
probably far from those who could assist them.

Some of the more important points in the two
narratives it is necessary, however briefly and
baldly, to notice.   (a) I cannot think that there

is a shadow of justification for regarding Luke i. 34, 35—the question of Mary, " How shall this be ? " and the answer of the angel—as an addition to the original document, inserted either by St. Luke himself or by some unknown interpolator, and for thus eliminating the idea of the Virgin-birth from the genuine Gospel. The authenticity of these verses is not, and cannot be, impugned on the ground of any lack of external evidence ; they have, from the point of view of textual criticism, as good a right to a place in the Gospel as any verses. The arguments brought forward against them are wholly subjective ; [1] and I hope that it is not arrogant to say that these arguments appear to me both far-fetched and mechanical. (b) St. Luke connects our Lord's birth at Bethlehem with peculiar circumstances created by the enrolment under Quirinius. On this subject of perennial controversy it must here be sufficient to say, *first*, that St. Luke is entitled to have taken into account that character for historical accuracy which the evidence of the Acts establishes ; *secondly*, that, while it cannot by any means be maintained that all difficulties have been cleared up, it is certainly true that the investigations of Professor Ramsay have advanced by many degrees the probability

[1] See the article of Professor Harnack in the *Zeitschrift für die neutestamentliche Wissenschaft*, 1901, p. 53 ff.

that St. Luke's reference to the enrolment is historical.   (c) It is said that St. Luke's assertion that Mary and Joseph did not understand the words of the Holy Child, " Wist ye not that I must be in my Father's house ? " (Luke ii. 49), is inconsistent with the story of the Annunciation. I do not myself feel the difficulty ; if I did, I should plead that the notice may well be one of those editorial comments, which are not infrequent in the Gospels, and which embody a common-place of the history.   (d) Unless the secret of the Lord's birth had been made widely known from the first, it was necessary that He should be regarded as Joseph's son, and that Joseph's genealogy should be accounted as His genealogy.   (e) It is difficult to see why the announcement of the Divine Sonship at the Baptism should be in conflict with the story of the supernatural birth, so that, as it is alleged, these two histories must be regarded as two independent methods of deifying a revered teacher.   It may be reverently asserted that it was psychologically natural (if the word ' natural ' may be used in such a connexion) that at a great spiritual crisis of His life our Lord should become conscious of His unique relation to the Father. (f) I have reserved for the last place the consideration of an important and difficult subject. The two narratives of our Lord's birth have one

F

characteristic in common, not peculiar indeed to
these sections of the Gospels but specially conspicuous in them. What are we to say of the
Angelic appearances which play so large a part
in these narratives ?   To some minds these mani-
festations cause no difficulty. But to others, who
are far indeed from denying the existence of
created spiritual beings, they are a stumbling-block
and seem to give an air of unreality to the history
in which they form incidents. The sight, for
example, and the sound of a multitude of the
heavenly host singing in the sky have nothing
analogous to them in the experiences of the most
spiritually-minded men in these days. The difficulty—and to some it is very real and oppressive—
is mitigated, even if it is not wholly removed, by
three considerations which are closely related to
each other. In the first place, to the mind of a
pious Jew the world around him was peopled with
spirits, good and bad ; and to him, therefore, an
intense spiritual impression, as we should say,
would naturally present itself as the message of
an angel, and he would with ' the eyes of the heart '
and so, in his own belief, with the eyes of the body
see angelic visitants. Secondly, we cannot but
think that Divine revelation is conditioned as to
its methods by the beliefs of those to whom it is
vouchsafed. Thirdly, some at least of these

details in the story may be due to the influence of poetic instinct and of the literature of the Old Testament in the case both of the Evangelists themselves and of those through whom the history came to them. Thus, the story is told in the Gospels in the form in which, if we assume its truth, it would naturally and perhaps inevitably shape itself in the minds and on the lips of the first actors and of those who heard them and repeated their tale.

But the question must be asked, How, on the supposition that the story of the Lord's birth is due to a mythopoeic tendency, are we to account for its genesis ?   In what circles did it originate ? And here a choice between two main alternatives is offered to us.   The story must on this assumption be the embodiment either of Gentile or of Jewish ideas.

" For the whole birth- and childhood-story of Matthew," writes Professor Usener,[1] " in its every detail it is possible to trace a pagan substratum. It must have arisen in Gentile-Christian circles, probably in the province of Asia, and then was to some extent legitimated by its narrator." " The Jewish-Christian representation of Luke," according to this theory, " had to be heightened by the introduction of the angelic messages and so

[1] *Encyclopaedia Biblica*, iii. 3352.

brought into conformity with the demands of
faith." Against such an hypothesis two objections,
decisive in my judgment, at once suggest themselves. In the first place, if time is to be found
for the complicated interaction between paganism
and Christianity which this theory involves, the
First and Third Gospels must be placed at a date
which, I believe, is quite untenable. In the
second place, the story in St. Matthew, like that
in St. Luke, moves within the circle of Eastern *Jewi-*
conceptions. Its Jewish character is not a veneer
which lies on the surface. The narrative is essentially Jewish. The solution, therefore, offered by
Professor Usener is directly at variance with the
primary conditions of the problem.

If the story is not a loan from paganism, it
must have grown up, if it be a romance, on Jewish
soil. Here three possible theories present themselves.

(1) The story has been regarded as the expan-
sion in a concrete form of the idea conveyed by
the mistranslation in the LXX. of the passage in
Isaiah (vii. 14)—" the virgin shall conceive, and
bear a son." But there appears to be absolutely
no evidence that this passage in Isaiah, so familiar
in this connexion to ourselves, was ever interpreted
by the Jews in a Messianic sense. It is easy to
understand how it might be adduced to illustrate

a history already current ; it is difficult to see how
it could be considered so relevant to Jesus the
Messiah as to lead to the fabrication of a particular
story about His birth.

(2) It is sometimes urged that the language
of Philo as to the birth of some of the heroes of
the Old Testament suggested the story of our
Lord's birth.[1]   Philo, pressing the words of the
Scriptural narratives and giving to those narratives an allegorical meaning, speaks of the birth
of these heroes as due to a Divine generation.
But Philo regards the whole transaction in each
case and all the persons concerned in it as con-
stituting a philosophical parable.   The several
characters symbolize different virtues.   There is
a great gulf between the Platonic mysticism of the
Alexandrian thinker and the simple and purely
Jewish ideas embodied in the Evangelical stories
of the Lord's birth.   The Christological language
of the Gospel of the Infancy closely resembles the

---

[1] See, *e.g.*, Dr. E. A. Abbott's article in the *Encyclopaedia
Biblica*, 1778.   The passages of Philo (ed. Mangey) referred
to are i. 131, 147 f., 215, 273, 598 f.   As an example of Philo's
method I quote the first of the above passages : " ' The Lord
created laughter for me ; for every one that heareth will
rejoice with me ' (Gen. xxi. 6, LXX.).   Open then wide your
ears, ye initiated, and receive sacred mysteries.   Laughter
is joy, and ' created ' is equivalent to ' begat,' so that the
words signify ' the Lord begat Isaac ' ; for He is the Father
of the perfect nature, sowing and gendering happiness in
souls."

Messianic language of the Psalms of Solomon and of the Eighteen Benedictions : [1] " He shall be great, and shall be called the Son of the Most High : and the Lord God shall give unto him the throne of his father David : and he shall reign over the house of Jacob for ever ; and of his kingdom there shall be no end " (Luke i. 32 f.). Such anticipations cannot be the invention of men who borrowed their ideas from Philo, with whom the Messianic hope had dwindled to a vanishing point.   Nor, on the other hand, can they be due, I will not say to the Gentile Evangelist, the friend of St. Paul, but to any believer in the Messiahship of Jesus in days when the Jews had rejected Him, and when the Resurrection and Ascension had raised the conception of His Messiahship to that of a spiritual and universal sovereignty.   The Christology of these chapters is a decisive proof that they are Palestinian in origin and absolutely primitive and even pre-Christian in character.

(3) A third alternative must be considered. Is the story of the Lord's birth a romance intended, in point of wonder and of Divine interposition, to raise His birth above the birth of Isaac, the child of promise, to which the birth of the Baptist is

---

[1] See Ryle and James, *The Psalms of Solomon*, Introduction, pp. xci. f. ; also my *The Lord's Prayer in the Early Church* (Texts and Studies, i. 3), pp. 147 ff.

analogous ? Such a theory at any rate would not be in conflict with the simple and non-pagan character of the narrative of the Evangelists. But two lines of thought are specially relevant here. In the first place, if we put aside the esoteric doctrines and practices of the Essenes, there is nothing which suggests that the Jews exalted virginity above the married state. Many passages of the Old Testament at once occur to our minds which indicate that Israel held marriage in special honour. The story of the Lord's birth is, we may say with confidence, alien in its very nature to Jewish ideas. In the second place, it was in large measure as a power making for truth that Christianity gained its victories. It was conspicuous as creating a new standard of truth : it set a new value on truth. In the first age it could not afford to be in conflict with its own first principles. Historical criticism cannot leave out of sight the influence of moral sentiment. A love of truth, reinforced by a deep sense of reverence for the Lord Jesus, cannot but have been a power restraining His disciples from taking liberties with the story of His earthly life. I know that there are many strange surprises in the history of religion. But I confess that I find it very hard to believe that in the inner circle of the earliest disciples at Jerusalem (*i.e.* within forty years after

the Passion) there grew up and took shape, not
poetical and idealized adjuncts to the story of the
Lord's birth, but a story itself wholly fictitious.

One objection of a more general character still
remains. The real difficulty which many feel has
been expressed in these words : " We should not
now expect, *a priori*, that the Incarnate Logos
would be born without a human father." [1] But
surely we can have no *a priori* expectations of any
kind as to the way in which the Incarnation would
be brought about.   We have no exact knowledge,
so far as I am aware, of the laws of heredity as
they affect moral character, or, in regard to the
entail of sinful propensities, of the relation of the
father's to the mother's influence.   Still less have
we any acquaintance with, or experience of, any
analogous event to inform and guide our ideas as
to the way in which " the Word became flesh."
We cannot say that it was necessary, however
congruous it may appear to many devout and
thoughtful minds, that the Word, when becoming
Incarnate, should be born of a Virgin mother.
Neither on the other hand can we assert that it
was natural that one who stands alone among
men, as being truly Divine as well as truly human,
should enter the world in the common way of

---

[1] *Contentio Veritatis*, p. 88.   Dr. Inge is giving a résumé
of the " difficulties which many people now feel."

human generation. A little reflection must convince us that we are not in a position to dogmatize as to what was either necessary or natural in relation to an event so uniquely unique as the Incarnation. In such a matter *a priori* assumptions in this direction or in that are emphatically irrelevant.

Two conclusions, from the point of view of historical criticism, seem to me to be beyond doubt. On the one hand it is not too much to assert that there are very serious difficulties as to the genesis of the story of our Lord's birth, if we give up its historical truth. On the other hand the evidence is slight. That must be candidly admitted. But to estimate the force of this admission we must ask the question—Can we, if the truth of the history is assumed, conceive of the evidence being essentially different from what it is ? We keep our birthdays ; we veil all that concerns the first beginning of our physical life in reverent silence. It cannot have been otherwise in the Holy Family. The story, if true, must have rested ultimately on the word of the Lord's mother. It can only have been known to very few, and their lips must have long been sealed.

The discussion of some of the most important among the problems which historical criticism raises as to the Gospels leads us finally to the question what is at the present time, and what in the future is likely to be, the effect of historical criticism on Christian belief.

One view of the general position finds expression in the following words of Dr. Rashdall : [1] " We may be quite confident that for minds which have once appreciated the principles of historical criticism, or minds affected by the diffused scepticism which has sprung from historical criticism, neither religious faith in general, nor any doctrine of primary religious importance, will ever depend mainly upon the evidence of abnormal events recorded to have happened in the remote past." To speak frankly, the attribution of such a result as this to the recognition of the principles of historical criticism appears to me to be legitimate only on the assumption *either* that the " abnormal events "—whether any event is in an absolute sense abnormal depends on its antecedents and environment—are of such a nature that historical criticism, if it has not done so already, must eventually pronounce clearly and decidedly a negative verdict, *or* that religious faith can only be based on demonstrated knowledge. The former of these assumptions is, to say the very least, premature. The latter neglects the lesson which is enforced

[1] *Contentio Veritatis*, p. 58.

on us by common experience, namely, that in departments of life which are of the deepest and most intimate concern to us we rest on probabilities, and we act on probabilities.   The theistic position itself is incapable of strict proof.   Though the science of history, as we have seen, cannot attain to other than probable conclusions as to an alleged event in the past, yet the probability of a given conclusion may be of so high a degree that theories and actions are legitimately based upon it on which, for instance, the welfare of a nation may depend.   The whole evidence, for example, for our Lord's Resurrection (I am not now referring to the details of the story of the Resurrection or of the appearances of the risen Lord), while of course it does not compel intellectual assent, does appear to be of such a nature as to form a secure foundation on which rational faith can repose, and on which religious philosophy can rationally build a superstructure of doctrine.

Yet without controversy the student of Christian doctrine is profoundly affected by the recognition of the validity of the principles of historical criticism.   " Several of these articles [*i.e.* of the Christian Creed] relate to historical facts, and our belief in these must be obtained by evidence of the same nature as that on which we believe

other historical facts. . . . It is impossible to
evolve a historical fact out of our inner consciousness, or to have any real belief that anything
took place 1800 years ago, merely because we wish
it did and because we find such a belief comforting
and consolatory "—so Dr. Salmon wrote nearly
a quarter of a century ago ; [1] and such a position
as this is becoming more and more a common-place
of educated religious thought. Our acceptance of
it must be no mere otiose assent : it must be real
and practical. It seems to me to involve three
chief consequences.

(1) It quickens the desire for truth as opposed
to an easy contentment with traditional ways of
thinking. The loyal seeker after truth is sure to
meet with perplexities and trials of faith ; he may
even be saddened by what at first appear to be
losses. That it is possible that he will find some
readjustments and some restatements needful,
cannot beforehand be absolutely and categorically
denied. But I at least believe that in the end he
will hold in reassured possession all that is deepest
and most fundamental in the orthodoxy of the
past.

(2) It will, I believe, be more and more clearly
seen that, in regard to the events of our Lord's life
on earth recorded in the Gospels, there is a wide

[1] *Non-miraculous Christianity*, p. 6.

difference between the amount and the nature of the evidence available in the several cases, and a corresponding difference between the degrees of certitude or (to speak strictly) of historical probability which can be attained. All evidence is not the same evidence. All belief is not the same belief. Christianity is an historical religion ; and therefore, as in the natural order, so in the world of faith there must needs be twilight as well as noontide splendour. Inability to rank all articles of the Creed on the same level in regard to historical evidence is not equivalent to the denial of any.

(3) The thoughtful Christian will recognise more clearly than in past days that he lives his religious life by faith, not by sight, not by that demonstrated certainty which in the intellectual sphere corresponds to sight. He will also be content to admit that round his central beliefs there lies a margin of admittedly open questions. The cry 'all or nothing' is the confession of despair. In his last letter, in answer to an invitation from his life-long friend Archbishop Benson to write a paper on Inspiration, Bishop Lightfoot said : " There is nothing so dangerous on such a topic as the desire to make everything right and tight. I do not know whether it is that my mind is illogical, but I find that my faith suffers nothing

by leaving a thousand questions open, so long as I am convinced on two or three main lines." [1]

In days like these a pre-eminent practical danger is lest, as at Alexandria at the close of the second century, so among ourselves there should grow up a feeling of alienation between those who (to adopt the phraseology of Clement) may be called simple believers and those who may be called Christian Gnostics. Such a temper is strictly schismatical, and sins against the unity of the Body of Christ. The one side must allow to an intellectual and spiritual movement, of which they themselves do not feel the need, reasonable freedom. Mistakes in the application of historical criticism to the records of the New Testament are sure to be made ; and in so serious a subject even trivial mistakes are serious. But the spirit of suspicion must be kept in check. The mistakes of an earnest seeker after truth must not be treated with harshness. It is certain that the criticism of those without cannot be satisfactorily dealt with, unless the criticism of those within is honest and courageous as well as cautious and reverent. The other side must see to it that the liberty which they rightly claim does not become license. The Church, like every other society, must define its

[1] *The Life of Edward White Benson*, ii. p. 289. The date of the letter is Dec. 14, 1889. The Bishop died on Dec. 21.

conditions of membership and of admission to office. At the heart of these lies the confession of the Apostles' Creed. No good can come from a light view of serious obligations. But quite apart from license in this extreme sense, nothing involves greater danger to the cause of Truth than rash, crude, defiant pronouncements on subjects which touch men's deep and sacred convictions. The Apostle's maxim " speaking truth in love " is binding on no one more conspicuously than on the Christian critic. The student must bring the results of his investigations, more or less certain, and submit them to those who are trained in the school of practical religious life. They must take their part in the progress towards a final verdict. The conclusions of the critical intellect must be reviewed, and, if need be, revised in the light of the widest experience and the fullest knowledge. For indeed the subject with which I have endeavoured to deal in this Essay is not the exclusive possession of the specialist. It is one in which the whole Christian Society is vitally concerned. To the whole Christian Society is given the promise of the Holy Spirit as a guide into " all the truth." Those who are called to be students and whose special duty it is—a difficult, anxious, and perilous duty—to examine these problems and to strive for their solution, need, no less than the evangelist and the missionary, the intercessions of their brethren that the Spirit of Truth may teach and control them, that they may be endued with the spirit of intellectual discernment and honesty and with the spirit of reverence and godly fear.

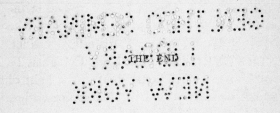

THE END

Printed by R. & R. Clark, Limited, *Edinburgh.*

BY THE BISHOP OF ELY

THE CREDIBILITY OF THE BOOK OF THE ACTS OF THE APOSTLES

HULSEAN LECTURES, 1900–1901.

Crown 8vo.   6s.

CONFIRMATION IN THE APOSTOLIC AGE

Globe 8vo.   2s. 6d. net.

THE SYRO-LATIN TEXT OF THE GOSPELS

8vo.   7s. 6d. net.

THE OLD SYRIAC ELEMENT IN THE TEXT OF THE CODEX BEZAE

8vo.   7s. 6d. net.

LONDON : MACMILLAN AND CO., LTD.